ISBN 978-1-333-94753-8
PIBN 10601308

1 MONTH OF
FREE
READING

at

www.ForgottenBooks.com

By purchasing this book you are eligible for one month membership to ForgottenBooks.com, giving you unlimited access to our entire collection of over 700,000 titles via our web site and mobile apps.

To claim your free month visit:

www.forgottenbooks.com/free601308

English
Français
Deutsche
Italiano
Español
Português

www.forgottenbooks.com

Mythology Photography **Fiction**
Fishing Christianity **Art** Cooking
Essays Buddhism Freemasonry
Medicine **Biology** Music **Ancient**
Egypt Evolution Carpentry Physics
Dance Geology **Mathematics** Fitness
Shakespeare **Folklore** Yoga Marketing
Confidence Immortality Biographies
Poetry **Psychology** Witchcraft
Electronics Chemistry History **Law**
Accounting **Philosophy** Anthropology
Alchemy Drama Quantum Mechanics
Atheism Sexual Health **Ancient History**
Entrepreneurship Languages Sport
Paleontology Needlework Islam
Metaphysics Investment Archaeology
Parenting Statistics Criminology
Motivational

COUNTIES

OF

ILLINOIS.

Their Origin and Evoluti

With Twenty-Three Maps Showing the Origina.

the Present Boundary Lines of Each

County in the State.

COMPILED AND PUBLISHED BY

JAMES A. ROSE, Secretary of State,

JANUARY 1, 1906.

COUNTIES

OF

ILLINOIS.

Their Origin and Evolution

With Twenty-Three Maps Showing the Original and
the Present Boundary Lines of Each
County of the State.

COMPILED AND PUBLISHED BY
JAMES A. ROSE, Secretary of State,
JANUARY 1, 1906.

SPRINGFIELD:
ILLINOIS STATE JOURNAL CO., STATE PRINTERS
1906

EXPLANATORY.

This pamphlet consists of an article entitled, "Counties of Illinois" extracted from the Illinois Blue Book of 1906. It is published in this form to render possible a more liberal distribution of it than the limited edition of the Blue Book will allow. Similar maps, so far as I am informed, have never before been published; and the text explanatory of the maps, has been compiled from original sources. The exact language of statutes and proclamations has been quoted except in some instances where, to economize space, abridgements have semed advisable; but no abridgement has been allowed to alter or obscure the meaning of the original.

JAMES A. ROSE,
Secretary of State.

Springfield, Jan. 1, 1906.

COUNTIES OF ILLINOIS.

The counties of Illinois are 102 in number of which McLean is the greatest in area with 1,161 square miles and Cook the most populous with 1,838,735 as returned by the federal census of 1900. Putnam is the smallest both in extent and population, having an area of 170 square miles and 4,706 inhabitants, McLean having about seven times its area and Cook about 400 times its population. Cook contains the greatest number of incorporated municipalities, fifty-nine; Vermilion the next in number, twenty-five; while Schuyler and Wabash contain the smallest number, two each.

For the purpose of the regulation of official fees and salaries the counties of the State are divided into three classes: Those of not more than 25,000 population (fifty-two in number), are of the first class; those of more than 25,000 and less than 100,000, (forty-nine in number), are of the second class; those of more than 100,000 are of the third class, Cook being the only county in this class.

The powers of the county as a body politic and corporate are exercised by the county board, which consists, in Cook county, of fifteen commissioners, ten elected from the city of Chicago and five from the outlying townships. In other counties under township organization the county board consists of the supervisors from the several townships of the county. In counties not under township organization, the county board consists of three commissioners elected by the electors of the entire county for a term of three years with terms so arranged that a new member will be elected each year.

The system of township organization provided by the statutes is optional with the several counties any one of which may change to or from such system by a majority vote of all the electors of the county. Elections for the adoption of township organization may be ordered on a petition of fifty electors and for the discontinuance of the systen on petition of one-fifth of the electors of the county. There are nineteen counties not under township organization.

County organization in Illinois dates back to 1779 when, after the conquest of Kaskaskia and Vincennes by George Rogers Clark in 1778, the "County of Illinois" was established by legislative enactment of Virginia and the new county, vaguely defined as to boundaries, was attached to that commonwealth. This was passed in October 1778 and proclamation of the act made June 17, 1779. Captain John Todd was appointed "County lieutenant commandent" and organized the government with the county seat at Kaskaskia. But the machinery of county government was never effectually set up, and it soon ceased to run.

St. Clair and Randolph as Counties of Northwest Territory.

In 1784, Virginia surrendered to the general government all claims to this territory and in 1787 "An Act for the government of the territory of the United States northwest of the Ohio river" was passed by the congress sitting under the articles of confederation. Under this ordinance General Arthur St. Clair was appointed governor of the territory, and, in 1790, organized by proclamation, the county of St. Clair, named in honor of himself.

4

To understand the boundaries defined in this and subsequent proclamations and in the early legislative acts setting up counties in the Northwest Territory, Indiana territory and the territory of Illinois, it is necessary to know the geographical location of a number of points not found on modern maps of Illinois. Some of these points are:

The "Little Michilimackinac"; the Mackinaw river flowing into the Illinois four or five miles below Pekin in Tazewell county.

"The little river above Fort Massac"; now called Massac creek, flowing in to the Ohio immediately east of the city of Metropolis, Massac county.

"Standing Stone Forks" of the Great Miami; near the present site of the village of Loramie, in the western part of Shelby county, Ohio.

"Theokiki river"; the Kankakee.

"Chicago river"; the DesPlaines.

"Cahokia"; the northeast part of town 1 north, 10 west, St. Clair county.

"Prairie du Rocher"; near the center of town 5 south, 9 west, Randolph county.

"Cave Spring" and "Sink Hole Spring"; believed to be identical and located in Monroe county, section ten, town four south, range ten west, about nine miles south and one mile west of the city of Waterloo.

"The Great Cave on the Ohio"; section thirteen, town twelve south, nine east of the third principal meridian, near the present village of Cave-in-Rock, Hardin county.

"The Great Kennomic," or "Kalamik," or "Calumet"; a small stream flowing into the southern bend of Lake Michigan in Lake county, Indiana, about eighteen miles east of the Illinois State line.

"Mile's Trace"; an old road or trail from Elizabethtown to Kaskaskia, a part of which led from the head waters of Lusk creek northwesterly through Crab Orchard and across the western line of Williamson county near its northern boundary.

"Lusk Creek"; a small stream still bearing that name, emptying into the Ohio immediately above the city of Golconda, Pope county.

"Gagnic Creek"; the DeGagnia, a small creek emptying into the Mississippi in town eight south, five west, on the present boundary line between Randolph and Jackson counties.

"Bompass", "Bompast" or "Bon Pas" creek or river; a small branch of the Wabash forming the present boundary between Edwards and Wabash counties.

"Boon's Mill"; west of the center of town 7 south, 10 east of the 3d principal meridian near the present site of New Haven.

The outlines of the latter counties formed after the territory had been brought under the federal system of surveys, with boundaries described by township and range lines, are easily traced.

1790—St Clair County

April 27, 1790, Governor St. Clair issued his proclamation organizing St. Clair as a county of the Northwest Territory. It had for its boundaries a direct line from the mouth of the Little Mackinaw to the mouth of the Massac creek, thence down the Ohio to the Mississippi, up the Mississippi to the mouth of the Illinois and up the Illinois to the mouth of the Mackinaw. As thus constituted the county extended nearly two hundred and fifty miles from north to south with a maximum width of about eighty miles. It embraced the territory of twenty existing counties and fractions of eleven others. But with all this wealth of territory, St. Clair was a small county as compared with Knox, created by proclamation June 20 of the same year, which included about half of the State of Illinois, the whole of Indiana, that part of Ohio west of the Great Miami river, the greater part of Michigan, and a considerable part of Wisconsin as these states exist at present. Knox was organized to meet the wants of the settlements about Vincennes. The outlines of St. Clair and of the Illinois portion of Knox are found on Map No. 1.

1795—RANDOLPH COUNTY.

October 5, 1795, Randolph county was created a county of the Northwest Territory by proclamation of Governor St. Clair and included all that part of the then existing county of St. Clair lying south of a line running from the Mississippi directly east through "the cave spring a little south of the New Design" settlement to the boundary of Knox county.· Assuming the "cave spring" mentioned in this proclamation to be identical with the "Sink Hole Spring" of Governor Harrison's later proclamations, this east and west line was about two miles south of the present southern boundary of St. Clair county. This division gave to Randolph about one third of the territory of St. Clair as first established. These boundaries, shown on Map No. 2, remained unchanged until after the organization of Indiana Territory in 1800.

1801—ST. CLAIR AND RANDOLPH AS COUNTIES OF INDIANA TERRITORY.

February 6. 1801, William Henry Harrison, Governor of the Territory of Indiana, issued his proclamation continuing the counties of St. Clair and Randolph as counties of Indiana Territory, but changed their boundaries and enlarged their areas. The east and west line dividing St. Clair and Randolph ran directly east from the Mississippi through the center of Sink Hole spring until it intersected a line drawn directly north from the "Great Cave on the Ohio." The point of intersection of these two lines is in section 12, town 4 south, 9 east, in White county and was made the northeast corner of Randolph county, the eastern boundary of Randolph being this line north from the cave, while the Ohio and Mississippi formed the southeastern and southwestern boundaries respectively. St. Clair, as defined by this proclamation, had for its eastern boundary a line drawn from the northeastern corner of Randolph to the "mouth of the Great Kennomic river," and for its northern boundary, the Canada line. By the terms of this proclamation but little Illinois territory—a narrow strip along the Wabash—was left in Knox county. St. Clair contained not only the greater part of the present State of Illinois, but all of Wisconsin and a considerable part of Michigan and Minnesota as well. St. Clair and Randolph as counties of Indiana Territory are shown on Map No. 3, except the part of St. Clair extending beyond the present limits of the State.

1803—ST. CLAIR AND RANDOLPH—BOUNDARIES CHANGED.

In response to sundry petitions, Governor Harrison re-adjusted by proclamation of March 25, 1803, the dividing line between Randolph and St. Clair. The dividing line thus established ran from a point on the Mississippi, about four miles further south than the old boundary, northeast to Sink Hole spring; thence in a northeasterly direction till it intersected a line running north from Cave-in-Rock. The point of intersection is in Jasper county, town six north, nine east of the third principal meridian, near the present site of Newton. The other boundaries of the two counties were unchanged and so remained until after the organization of the Territory of Illinois in 1809. This change of boundary is shown on Map No. 4.

· 1809—ST. CLAIR AND RANDOLPH AS COUNTIES OF ILLINOIS TERRITORY.

April 28, 1809, Nathaniel Pope, Secretary and Acting Governor of the new territory, issued his proclamation continuing St. Clair and Randolph counties of Illinois Territory without change of boundaries, except that the eastern boundary of each county was extended to the eastern boundary of Illinois Territory, now the eastern boundary of the State. This gave to Randolph additional territory on the east and to St. Clair a triangular strip along the southern part and took from it a triangular strip from the northern part of its eastern side, and eliminated Knox county from Illinois Territory. St. Clair still extended north to the Canada line. Map No. 5 shows St. Clair and Randolph as the two original counties of Illinois Territory as re-established in 1809. ·

1812—MADISON, GALLATIN AND JOHNSON.

September 12, 1812, by proclamation of Governor Ninian Edwards, three new counties, Madison, Gallatin and Johnson, were created. Madison included all that part of the territory of Illinois lying north of the present southern boundary of Madison extended to the Wabash. Gallatin was bounded on the north by this same line, on the east by the Wabash and Ohio rivers and on the west and southwest by the Big Muddy, Miles's trace and Lusk creek. Johnson included all the territory bounded by the Big Muddy, Mississippi and Ohio rivers, Lusk creek and Miles's trace. This proclamation cut St. Clair down to comparatively small dimensions and made of it the smallest county of the Territory. These were the last counties created by proclamation. In this year Illinois was raised to the second grade of territorial government, and the creation of new counties and alteration of county lines devolved, thereafter, upon the Territorial Legislature. The outlines of these counties are shown on Map No. 6.

1813—BOUNDARIES READJUSTED.

December 11, 1813, two acts were passed by the first Territorial Legislature readjusting the boundary lines of St. Clair, Randolph and Gallatin. The line running northeasterly from Sink Hole spring as the southeastern boundary of St. Clair was abandoned and Sink Hole spring lost its importance as a landmark. Lines of the Federal survey had been established by this time, and the line between townships three and four south (extended from the Mississippi to the third principal meridian) was made the dividing line between St. Clair and Randolph. The third principal meridian from the southern boundary of Madison to its intersection with Miles's trace was made the dividing line between Gallatin to the east and St. Clair and Randolph to the west. By these acts, those parts of St. Clair and Randolph east of the third principal meridian were added to Gallatin, nearly half of the remaining territory of Randolph was added to St. Clair and a small triangle from the extreme southwestern part of St. Clair was added to Randolph. Madison and Johnson remained unchanged. The county boundaries established by these acts are shown on Map No. 7.

1814-1815—EDWARDS AND WHITE.

Nov. 20, 1814, the Territorial Legislature passed "An act for the division of Gallatin county," which act divided Madison county as well, and from the northern part of Gallatin and the part of Madison lying east of the third principal meridian, made Edwards the sixth county of the territory. Dec. 9, 1815, Gallatin was further reduced by the creation of White including besides the present area of White all the territory directly west of it to the third principal meridian. These two counties are shown on Map No. 8.

1816—MONROE, JACKSON, POPE AND CRAWFORD.

Jan. 6, 1816, Monroe county was created, Jackson and Pope Jan. 10, and Crawford Dec. 31, of the same year. Monroe, from St. Clair and Randolph, was given substantially its present boundaries except that the eastern boundary across town 3 has since been carried east to the Kaskaskia river. Several changes have since been made in the northeastern and southeastern boundaries of Monroe, but all of a trifling character. Jackson, from Randolph, included besides its present area, the southern part of the present county of Perry. Pope, from Johnson and Gallatin, contained besides its present area, portions of the present counties of Massac, Johnson and Hardin. Dec. 8 of the same year the northeastern boundary of Pope was carried east six miles, that is to a line running from the "Rock and Cave" (Cave-in-Rock) on the Ohio to the southwest corner of town 10 south, 8 east. Crawford included all that part of the territory lying east of the third principal meridian, and north of the line dividing towns 3 and 4 north. That part of Johnson between Miles's trace and the third principal meridian was attached temporarily, the eastern part to Gallatin and the western part to Jackson. These changes of county lines are shown on Map No. 9.

Jan. 4, 1817, Bond county was created, a parallelogram twenty-four miles wide from east to west and about 600 miles in length, reaching from a line six miles south of its present southern boundary to Lake Superior on the north. The Illinois part of this county is shown on Map No. 10.

1818—FRANKLIN, UNION AND WASHINGTON.

By acts of Jan. 2, 1818, three new counties were created, the last counties of territorial origin. Franklin included, besides its present area, all of Williamson. Union was given its present territory to which was temporarily attached the country lying south of it and between the Mississippi and Ohio rivers. Union was the first county of Illinois to which was given its present boundaries. Washington, formed from the eastern part of St. Clair, included, besides its present area, the greater part of the present county of Clinton. Map No. 11 shows the counties of Illinois as they existed at the close of the territorial period. The admission of Illinois as a State in 1818 worked no change in county boundaries except that Madison, Bond and Crawford no longer extended north to the Canada line, but had for their northern limit the present northern boundary of the State.

1819—ALEXANDER, CLARK, JEFFERSON AND WAYNE.

The second session of the first General Assembly of the State created four new counties, Alexander, Clark, Jefferson and Wayne. Alexander, (March 4) from unorganized territory south of Union, included besides its present area, a portion of Pulaski. Clark, (March 22) from the north part of Crawford, extended from the third principal meridian to the Indiana state line and from the present southern county boundary to the Wisconsin state line on the north. Jefferson, (March 26) from Edwards and White, included, besides its present area, the greater part of Marion. Wayne, (March 26) from Edwards, contained its present territory together with the southern part of Clay and the western part of Richland. Map No. 12 shows the county boundaries as they existed at the close of the first General Assembly of the State.

1821—LAWRENCE, GREENE, SANGAMON, PIKE, HAMILTON AND MONTGOMERY.

In 1821, six new counties were created. Lawrence, (January 16) from Crawford and Edwards, included, besides its present area, the greater part of Richland just west of it. Greene, (January 20) from Madison, included, besides its present area, that of Jersey. The unorganized territory to the north and east of Greene was temporarily attached to it. Sangamon, (January 30) from Madison and Bond, included, besides its present area, all of the existing counties of Cass, Menard, Logan, Mason, Tazewell, and parts of Christian, Macon, McLean, Woodford, Marshall and Putnam. Pike, (January 31) from Madison, Bond and Clark, included all that part of the State north and west of the Illinois and north of the Kankakee. Hamilton, (February 8) from the western part of White, was given its present boundaries and White was reduced to its existing limits. Montgomery, (February 12) from Bond and Madison, extended north from its present southern boundary to the county of Sangamon and included the southwestern part of Christian county. Town 10 and part of town 9 north, 1 west have since been added to Montgomery. Vandalia having been fixed upon as the future capital of the State, it was considered necessary to surround it with a county of suitable dimensions, and Fayette (February 14) was created from Bond, Jefferson, Wayne, Crawford and Clark. It had for its southern boundary the line dividing townships 2 and 3 north, and extended north 180 miles, to the Illinois river. It was 42 miles wide for a distance of 60 miles and 36 miles the remaining 120 miles of its extent. It contained nearly 7,000 square miles of territory and included within its boundaries, in whole or in part, 18 counties as they exist today. A strict construction of the act creating Fayette would have made its entire western boundary the line between ranges 1 and 2 west of the third principal meridian, and its northern boundary the Wisconsin state line; thus taking, south of the Illinois river, one range of townships from the east side of Sangamon (formed January 30) and, north of the river, cutting in two Pike (formed January 31), and making its area about 11,000 square miles. It is probable, however, that the word "unorganized" should be read into the first section of the act, making it read, "all that tract of *unorganized*" country lying north" etc. Subsequent acts seem to agree with this construction. The outlines of these counties are shown on Map No. 13.

1823—EDGAR, MARION, FULTON AND MORGAN.

In 1823, four new counties were created. Edgar, (January 3) from Clark, was given its present boundaries and unorganized territory north and west of it was temporarily attached to it. Marion, (January 24) from Fayette and Jefferson, was given its present boundaries. Fulton, (January 28) from Pike, included besides its present area, parts of Knox, Peoria and Schuyler, and the unorganized territory to the north and east was temporarily attached. Morgan, (January 31) from Sangamon and the unorganized territory north of Greene, included the present counties of Morgan, Scott and Cass. The boundaries of Pike were re-defined, restricting it to the territory between the Illinois and Mississippi south of a line drawn west from the present site of Beardstown. It contained the present counties of Pike and Calhoun, a small part of Schuyler and the greater part of Brown and Adams. The unorganized territory west of Fulton and north of Pike was temporarily attached to Pike. For these changes of boundary see Map No. 14.

1824—CLAY, CLINTON AND WABASH.

In 1824, three new counties were created. Clay, (December 23) from Fayette. Crawford and Wayne, included besides its present area, parts of Jasper and Richland. Clinton and Wabash, (December 27) the former from Washington, Fayette and Bond, and the latter from Edwards, were given their present boundaries. These acts also reduced Edwards, Wayne and Washington to their present limits. These changes of boundaries are shown on Map No. 15.

1825—TEN NEW COUNTIES.

In 1825, ten new counties were added, all of them in the territory north and west of the Illinois river: Calhoun (January 10), Adams, Hancock, Henry, Knox, Mercer, Putnam, Schuyler and Warren by a single act of January 13, and Peoria by a separate act of the same date. These acts gave to Adams, Hancock and Calhoun their present boundaries, included with Warren the present county of Henderson, gave to Mercer besides its present area, the part of Rock Island to the north of it, to Knox an area smaller by four townships than it now has, included with Schuyler the present county of Brown, and gave to Putnam all the unorganized country north of the Illinois and Kankakee rivers. Pike, Peoria and Fulton were reduced to their present limits. Hancock was attached to Adams, and Mercer to Schuyler, until the organization of these attached counties could be completed. The northern line of Sangamon was redefined and the detached portion temporarily attached to Fulton. A considerable tract of the unorganized territory east of Greene was added to Madison. Henry county extended south from the Wisconsin line to a line six miles south of its present boundary and from the 4th principal meridian east to the line dividing ranges 4 and 5. In defining Henry county, the Mississippi was not named as part of its western boundary, and as described in the act it extended beyond the Mississippi and included a considerable part of Iowa territory. The eastern boundary of Monroe county was carried east so as to include township 3 south, 8 west, from St. Clair, and in 1827 was further extended to the Kaskaskia river, adding to it the fractional township 3 south, 7 west from St. Clair, thus enlarging Monroe and reducing St. Clair to existing limits. The changes described are shown on Map No. 16.

1826—VERMILION AND McDONOUGH.

In 1826, but two new counties were established: Vermilion, (January 18) from unorganized territory attached to Edgar; and McDonough, with its present boundaries, from territory attached to Schuyler. These two counties are shown on Map No. 17. The unorganized territory north and west of Vermilion was temporarily attached to that county. Mercer and Warren were attached to Peoria, and McDonough to Schuyler, until their respective organizations could be completed.

1827—SHELBY, PERRY, TAZEWELL AND JoDAVIESS.

In 1827, four new counties were established: Shelby, (January 23) from Fayette, including its present territory and portions of Moultrie and Christian; Perry, (January 29) from Randolph and Jackson, was given its present boundaries; Tazewell, (January 31) from the unorganized territory east of the Illinois, included the present counties of Tazewell and Woodford and parts of McLean, Livingston, DeWitt, Logan and Mason; JoDaviess (February 17) from Mercer, Henry and Putnam, included a large area north of the "military tract" and west of the range line between 10 and 11 east of the 4th principal meridian including besides the present county of JoDaviess, four entire counties and parts of five others. The country north. of Shelby (formerly a part of Fayette) was temporarily attached to Shelby, that still further north to Tazewell and that north of Tazewell to Peoria. Mercer was reduced to its present limits: but, not having completed its organization, remained, with Warren, attached to Peoria. A small tract from St. Clair, lying west of the Kaskaskia was added to Monroe January 9. The county boundaries at the close of 1827 are shown on Map No. 18.

1829–1831—NINE NEW COUNTIES.

During this period nine new counties were created: Two in 1829, two in 1830 and five in 1831. In 1829, Macoupin, (January 17) from Madison and unorganized territory attached to Greene, was given its present boundaries, and Macon, (January 19) from territory attached to Shelby, included the present area of Macon, together with portions of Piatt, Moultrie and DeWitt.

In 1830; Coles, (December 25) from the western part of Clark and the unorganized territory north of it, included the present counties of Douglas, Coles and Cumberland. McLean, (December 25) from the eastern part of Tazewell and territory east of it, included all its present area with parts of Piatt, DeWitt, Logan, Woodford and Livingston.

In 1831, Cook, (January 15) from Putnam, contained, besides its present territory, all of Lake and DuPage and parts of McHenry and Will. LaSalle, (January 15) from Putnam and unorganized territory south of the Illinois, contained, besides its present area, all of Grundy and parts of Livingston, Kendall and Marshall. Rock Island, (February 9) from JoDaviess, was given its present boundaries. Effingham and Jasper, (February 15) were given their present boundaries, the first from Fayette and Crawford, and the latter from Crawford and Clay. The boundaries of Henry, Putnam and Knox were altered but neither county reduced to its present lines, Mercer was attached to Warren until fully organized; Henry was attached to Knox, and the unorganized country north of LaSalle was attached to that county. Towns 12 and 13 north, 5 east of the 4th principal meridian were included by acts of the same date in both Knox and Henry counties. The section of the act including this tract in Henry was repealed March 4, 1837. The county boundaries at the close of this period are shown on Map No. 19.

1833–1835—CHAMPAIGN AND IROQUOIS.

In 1833, Champaign, (February 20) from Vermilion and unorganized territory lying west of it, was given its present boundaries. Iroquois, (February 26) from unorganized territory north of Vermilion, included, besides its present area, nearly all of Kankakee and nearly half of Will. By these two acts Vermilion was reduced to its present limits. The boundary between Franklin and Perry was re-adjusted, (March 1, 1835) making Little Muddy river the dividing line between the counties. Feb 12, 1835, the line dividing Sangamon and Morgan was re-defined and provision made for its survey. In 1833, (February 26) Vermilion was enlargéd to its present limits by the addition of unorganized territory on the north. These changes are shown on Map No. 20.

1836—SIX NEW COUNTIES.

In 1836, six new counties were formed: Will, (January 12) from Cook and Iroquois, included, besides its present area, the part of Kankakee county lying north of the Kankakee river. Kane, McHenry, Ogle, Whiteside and Winnebago were created by a single act, (January 16). Kane included the present counties of Kane and DeKalb and part of Kendall; McHenry, besides its present area, included Lake; Winnebago included Boone and part of Stephenson; Ogle consisted of the present counties of Ogle and Lee, while Whiteside was given its present boundaries. The boundary of JoDaviess was re-defined and the area greatly reduced by the act of Jan 16. Winnebago, Ogle and Whiteside were attached to JoDaviess, and Kane to LaSalle, until their several organizations could be completed. See Map No. 21.

1837-1839—TWENTY-ONE NEW COUNTIES.

The changes made in the county boundaries in 1837 and 1839 are shown on Map No. 22.

In 1837, six new counties were created; Livingston (Feb. 27) from LaSalle, McLean and unorganized territory to the east; Bureau (Feb. 28) from Putnam; Cass,(March 3)from Morgan; Boone,(March 4) from Winnebago; DeKalb,(March 4) from Kane; and Stephenson,(March 4) from Winnebago and JoDaviess. All these were given their present boundaries except Cass, whose southern boundary was fixed three miles further north than now, and Winnebago was reduced to its present limits.

In 1839, fifteen new counties were formed, a greater number than in any other year of the State's history, and equal to all that have since been created. Marshall, (Jan. 9) from Putnam, was given its present boundaries, except that two townships (29 and 30 north, 1 east; from LaSalle) were attached in 1843; Brown, (Feb. 1) from Schuyler; DuPage, (Feb. 9) from Cook; and Dane remained Christian, (Feb. 15 and 26) from Shelby, Montgomery and Sangamon was given their present boundaries. Logan, (Feb. 15) from Sangamon, was smaller than at present, three whole and three fractional townships from Tazewell, (1840) and a fractional township from DeWitt, (1845) having since been added to the north. Menard, (Feb. 15) from Sangamon, included, besides its present area, about half of Mason county. Scott, (Feb. 16) from Morgan; Carroll, (Feb. 22) from JoDaviess; Lee, (Feb. 27) from Ogle; Jersey, (Feb 28) from Greene, and Williamson,(Feb. 28) from Franklin, were given their present boundaries. DeWitt,(March 1) from McLean and Macon, included, besides its present area; the northern part of Piatt and a small tract since attached to Logan. Lake, (March 1) from McHenry, was given its present boundaries. Hardin,(March 2) from Pope contained but about one half its present area; and Stark,(March 2) from Knox and Putnam, was given its present boundaries. Those several acts reduced the following ten counties to their present limits: Cook, Franklin, Green, JoDaviess, Knox, McHenry, Montgomery, Putnam, Sangamon and Schuyler. The western boundary of Hardin was changed Jan. 8, 1840, from the Grand Pierre creek to the present line between Pope and Hardin. The name of Dane county was changed to Christian Feb. 1, 1840.

1841-1859—FIFTEEN NEW COUNTIES.

Since 1839 fifteen new counties have been created, making the total number at the present time 102. No new counties have been created since 1859 and no important changes made in county boundaries since that year. Map No. 23 shows the county boundaries as they exist at the present time with the date of the formation of each.

In 1841 Henderson, (January 20) from Warren; Mason from Tazewell and Menard; Piatt, (January 27) from DeWitt and Macon; Grundy, (February 17) from La Salle; Kendall, (February 19) from La Salle and Kane; Richland, (February 24) from Clay and Lawrence; and Woodford, (February 27) from McLean and Tazewell, were given their present boundaries, and the following eight counties, Clay, Kane, La Salle, Lawrence, McLean, Menard, Tazewell and Warren, were reduced to their present limits.

In 1843, four new counties were created: Massac, (February 8) from Pope and Johnson; Moultrie, (February 16) from Shelby and Macon; Cumberland, (March 2) from Coles; and Pulaski, (March 3) from Johnson and Alexander, were given their present boundaries. Pope, Johnson, Shelby, Macon and Alexander were reduced to their present limits.

In 1845, (February 16) part of Morgan was added to Cass; (February 26) part of DeWitt was added to Logan; the line between Fulton and Peoria was re-adjusted (February 28), but no new counties were created.

In 1847, Saline, (February 25) from Gallatin, was given its present boundaries and (February 20) territory was added to Hardin. By these two acts, Gallatin was reduced to its present limits, and with the act of January 8, 1840, changing the eastern boundary of Pope, Hardin was given its present boundaries.

In 1856, Kankakee, (February 11) from Iroquois and Will, was given its present boundaries except that two townships (30 and 21 north, 9 east), were added to the western part, February 14, 1855. The act creating Kankakee reduced Iroquois and Will to their present limits.

In 1859, Douglas, (February 8) from Coles, was given its present boundaries and Coles reduced to its present limits; Ford, (February 17) the latest county to be created was formed from unorganized territory which had been attached to Vermilion since the creation of that county in 1826. Ford was given its present boundaries and Vermilion reduced to its present limits.

During this period and in preceding years as well, a number of laws affecting county boundaries were enacted which have not been referred to in this article for the reason that the changes made by these acts have been so unimportant that they could not well be shown on maps so small as those following this sketch and intendimg to illustrate it. Some of the lines on the maps are not beyond possible controversy. The acts establishing the lines are not always clear and are sometimes plainly contradictory. When Crawford was established in 1816, its western boundary was described as "the meridian"; and it has been assumed that the 3rd principal meridian was meant. The act creating Fayette in 1821, strictly construed. extended its northern limit to the Wisconsin line; but subsequent acts indicate that no territory north of the Illinois river was at any time considered a part of Fayette. The act of 1825 adding territory to Madison is contradictory in its terms and a subsequent act, reciting how this act shall not be construed, fails to clarify the original law. The provisions by which unorganized territory was "attached" to organized counties very greatly in terms, and possibly in meaning. Such territory is "temporarily attached" by one act "attached for county purposes" by another, for "judicial purposes" by a third. and still other forms are used. One act provides that property in the attached territory shall not be taxed for the erection of public buildings in the county to which the territory is attached. and another that "the inhabitants residing therein shall enjoy all the rights and privileges belonging to the citizens of the county" to which the territory is attached The act creating Fulton in 1823 gave to it definite boundaries as shown on Map No. 14, and declared that this territory "shall constitute a separate county"; but further declared that all the county east of the 4th meridian and north of the Illinois, formerly a part of Pike, "shall be attached to and be a part of said county until otherwise disposed of by the General Assembly", and it remained so attached until disposed of in 1825 by the creation of Peoria and Putnam counties. So it seems an open question whether the boundaries of Fulton for 1823 should be represented as on Map No. 14, or whether the county should be shown as reaching east from the 4th meridian to Lake Michigan, and north from the Illinois river to the Wisconsin line. Many such problems present themselves in considering these maps. But reference is made in each case to the act establishing the county and the interested reader may readily consult the creative act and reconstruct the map to correspond with his interpretation of its meaning. The purpose of the maps and of the descriptive matter accompanying them is to give to those interested in this branch of the State's history, a reasonably correct idea of the evolution of the counties of Illinois. It is believed that the maps are substantially correct and that few material errors will be found in the text explaining them.

Besides the 102 counties above enumerated, 13 other counties with names assigned and boundaries fixed, have been authorized by legislative enactment but failed to complete their organizations under the several enabling acts creating them: The counties of Coffee and Michigan in 1837; Allen and Okaw in 1841; Audubon, Benton, Marquette and Milton in 1843; Highland in 1847; Oregon in 1851; Harrison in 1855; Holmes in 1857 and Lincoln in 1867. Coffee, (March 1, 1837) was identical in boundaries with Stark, except that it contained one more township, now the southeastern township of Henry. Michigan, (March 2, 1837) contained, besides the present territory of DuPage county, that part of Cook lying north of DuPage and south of Lake and McHenry. Audubon (February 6, 1843) consisted of a rectangular tract, south of Christian county, running 12 miles south and 15 miles west, from the southeast corner of Christian and included parts of the present counties of Shelby, Fayette and Montgomery. Okaw (February 4, 1841) was almost identical in area with the present county of Moultrie, but extended three miles further west, and the zig-zag line forming its southwestern boundary was somewhat different. Marquette, (February 11, 1843) from Adams county, included townships 1 and 2 north and 1, 2 and 3 south, ranges 5 and 6 west of the 4th principal meridian, with six sections off the east side of township 1 south, 7 west. Highland (February 27, 1847) included all the territory assigned to Marquette in 1843, together with the eastern third of townships 1 and 2 north, 7 west and six additional sections from township 1 south, 7 west. Allen, Benton and Oregon included much territory in common from the southwestern part of Sangamon, the southeastern part of Morgan and the northern part of Macoupin. Allen (February 27, 1841) contained townships 12, 13, 14 and south half of 15 north, ranges 7 and 8 west; 12 and 13 and part of 14, range 9; and the western third of 12 north, 6 west. It took nearly an equal amount of territory from each of the three counties of Macoupin, Sangamon and Morgan. Benton (March 4, 1843) extended further west and south than Allen, but not so far east; its eastern boundary being the line between Morgan and Sangamon counties. Compared with Allen it took more territory from Morgan, less from Macoupin, a considerable tract from the northeastern part of Greene and none from Sangamon, but gained nearly enough from Morgan and Greene to balance the loss from Sangamon. Oregon (February 15, 1851) was very similar in outline to the old county of Allen, formed ten years earlier, but extended further east, taking in township 13 north, 6 west, and the eastern two-thirds of 12 north, 6 west, and its northern boundary extended a mile further north than that of Allen.

Another group of proposed counties in the eastern part of the State also covered much territory in common. Milton, (February 21, 1843) from the southern part of Vermilion county, included nearly one-third of the area of that county. Harrison, (February 14, 1855) mostly from the eastern part of McLean, included also portions of the present counties of Ford and Champaign. Holmes, (January 15, 1837) similar in shape to the present county of Ford, but larger in area, reaching twelve miles further north, six miles further south and three miles further east along its southern boundary, contained, besides the present area of Ford, portions of Kankakee, Champaign and Vermilion. Lincoln (March 9, 1867) occupied a strip from two to eight miles wide and thirty-six miles in length, along the eastern side of Champaign, and a somewhat wider strip of the same length from the western side of Vermilion. This included a part of the territory assigned to Milton in 1843 and to Holmes in 1857, as Holmes had included a part of Harrison formed in 1855.

COUNTIES OF ILLINOIS---DATES OF FORMATION.

1790. St. Clair, April 27.
1795. Randolph. October 5.
1812. Gallatin, Johnson and Madison, September 14.
1814. Edwards, November 28.
1815. White, December 9.
1816. Monroe, January 6; Jackson and Pope, January 10; Crawford, December 31.
1817. Bond, January 4.
1818. Franklin, Union and Washington. January 2.
1819. Alexander, March 4; Clark, March 22; Jefferson and Wayne, March 26.
1821. Lawrence, January 16; Greene, January 20; Sangamon, January 30; Pike, January 31; Hamilton, February 8; Montgomery, February 12; Fayette February 14.
1823. Edgar, January 3; Marion, January 24; Fulton, January 28; Morgan, January 31.
1824. Clay, December 23; Clinton and Wabash. December 27.
1825. Calhoun, January 10; Adams, Hancock, Henry, Knox, Mercer, Peoria, Putnam, Schuyler and Warren, January 13.
1826. Vermilion, January 18; McDonough, January 25.
1827. Shelby, January 23; Perry, January 29; Tazewell, January 31; Jo-Daviess, February 27.
1829. Macoupin, January 17; Macon, January 19.
1830. Coles and McLean, December 25.
1831. Cook and LaSalle, January 15; Rock Island, February 9; Effingham and Jasper, February 15.
1833. Champaign, February 20; Iroquois, February 26.
1836. Will, January 12; Kane, McHenry, Ogle, Whiteside and Winnebago, January 16.
1837. Livingston, February 27; Bureau, February 28; Cass, March 3; Boone, DeKalb and Stephenson, March 4.
1839. Marshall, January 19; Brown, February 1; DuPage, February 9; Christian, Logan and Menard, February 15; Scott. February 16; Carroll, February 22; Lee, February 27; Jersey and Williamson, February 28; DeWitt and Lake, March 1; Hardin and Stark, March 2.
1841. Henderson. Mason and Piatt, January 20; Grundy, February 17; Kendall, February 19; Richland, February 24; Woodford, February 27.
1843. Massac, February 8; Moultrie, February 16; Cumberland, March 2; Pulaski, March 3.
1847. Saline. February 25.
1853. Kankakee, February 11.
1859. Douglas, February 8; Ford, February 17.

[NOTE—The dates given above are the dates on which the proclamation was issued or the act approved without reference to the time of taking effect.]

1790—ST. CLAIR AND KNOX.

As counties of the Northwest Territory.

April 27—County of ST. CLAIR set off as follows: Beginning at the mouth of the Little Michilmacinack river, running thence southerly in a direct line to the mouth of the little river above Fort Massac, on the Ohio river; thence with the Ohio to its junction with the Mississippi; thence with the Mississippi to the mouth of the Illinois river; and so up the Illinois river to the place of beginning, with all the adjacent islands of the said Illinois and Mississippi rivers. St. Clair county divided into three judicial districts, viz.: Cahokia, Prairie du Rocher, and Kaskaskia; in each of which sessions of the several courts should be held during he year in the same manner as if each district represented a distinct county.
[Territorial Records of the Northwest Territory, St. Clair Papers, volume 2, page 165.]

June 20—A county named KNOX was laid off with the following boundaries: Beginning at the Standing Stone Forks of the Great Miami river and down the said river to the confluence with the Ohio river; thence with the Ohio river to the small stream or rivulet above Fort Massac; thence with the eastern line of St. Clair county to the mouth of the Little Michilmacinack; thence up the Illinois river to the forks or confluence of the Theokiki [Kankakee] and Chicago [Des Plaines]; thence by a line to be drawn due north to the boundary of the Territory of the United States, and so far easterly upon said boundary line as that a due south line may be drawn to the place of beginning.
[Territorial Records of the Northwest Territory, St. Clair Papers, volume 2, page 166.]

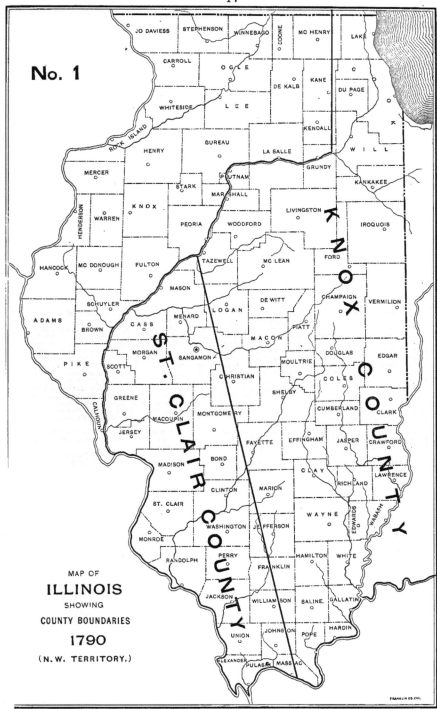

No. 1

MAP OF
ILLINOIS
SHOWING
COUNTY BOUNDARIES
1790
(N. W. TERRITORY.)

1795—RANDOLPH.

As a county of the Northwest Territory.

A PROCLAMATION.

Whereas, the division of the county of St. Clair into districts has not been found to give that ease and facility to the administration of justice which was expected, and the great extent of the country would render it almost impracticable were the courts to be held at one place only, it has, therefore, become necessary that it should be divided and a new county erected. Now, know ye, that by virtue of the power vested in me by the United States, I have ordered and ordained, and by these presents, do order and ordain, that all and singular, the lands lying and being within the following boundaries, viz: Beginning at the Cave spring, a little south of the New Design, and running thence due east to the line of the county of Knox, and thence south with that line to the Ohio river, thence with the Ohio to the Mississippi, thence with the Mississippi to the parallel of the said Cave spring, and thence to the place of beginning, shall be a county named and hereafter to be known and called by the name of RANDOLPH, which said county of Randolph shall have and enjoy, all and singular, jurisdiction and rights, liberties and immunities whatsoever to a county appertaining, and which any county that now is or hereafter may be erected and laid out shall or ought to enjoy conformably to the ordinance of Congress for the government of the Territory northwest of the river Ohio, bearing date the 15th day of July, 1787.

In testimony, I have hereunto set my hand and caused the seal of the Territory to be affixed, at Cahokia, in the county of St. Clair, the 5th day of October, in the year of our Lord 1795, and of the Independence of the United States the twentieth.

ARTHUR ST. CLAIR.

[Territorial records of the Northwest Territory. St. Clair papers. Vol. 2, p. 345.]

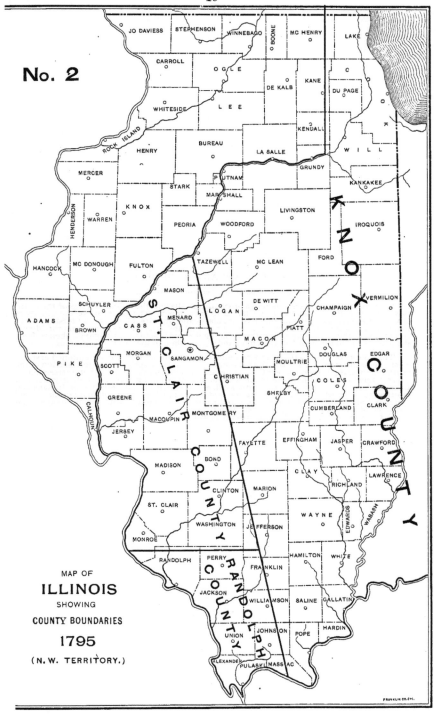

No. 2

MAP OF
ILLINOIS
SHOWING
COUNTY BOUNDARIES
1795
(N. W. TERRITORY.)

1801 ST. CLAIR AND RANDOLPH.

As counties of the Territory of Indiana.

February 3—The Governor issued a proclamation altering the boundary lines of the counties of Knox and Randolph and St. Clair as follows, towit: The boundary of the County of RANDOLPH shall begin on the Ohio river at a place called the Great Cave below the Saline Lick, thence by a direct north line until it intersects an east and west line running from the Mississippi through the Sink Hole spring, thence along the said line to the Mississippi, thence down the Mississippi to the mouth of the Ohio, and up the Ohio to the place of beginning.

The County of ST.CLAIR shall be bounded on the south by the before mentioned east and west line running from the Mississippi. through the Sink Hole spring to the intersection of the north line running from the Great Cave aforesaid, thence from the said point of intersection by a direct line to the mouth of the great Kennoumic river falling into the southerly bend of Lake Michigan, thence by a direct northeast line to the division line between the Indiana and Northwestern Territories, thence along the said line to the Territorial boundary of the United States and along the said boundary line to the intersection thereof with the Mississippi, and down the Mississippi to the place of beginning.
[Executive Journal of Indiana Territory, p. 98.]

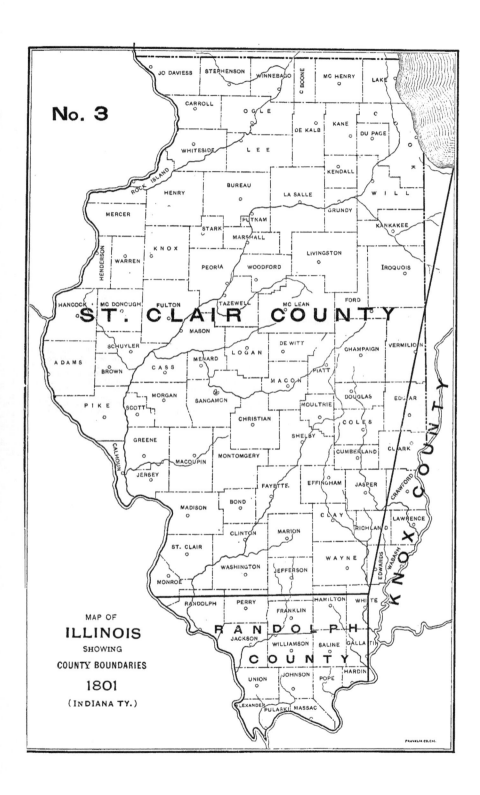

No. 3

MAP OF
ILLINOIS
SHOWING
COUNTY BOUNDARIES
1801
(INDIANA TY.)

1803—ST. CLAIR AND RANDOLPH.

As counties of Indiana Territory; boundaries changed.

March 25—Sundry petitions having been presented to the Governor from a number of the citizens of the County of Randolph, complaining of the great distance from the seat of Justice of their county, and praying that the line dividing the counties of Randolph and St. Clair may be so altered as to annex them to the latter, the Governor issued a proclamation declaring the line separating the counties of Randolph and St. Clair shall begin on the Mississippi river four miles and thirty-two chains south of the point where the present division line intersects the Mississippi Bottom, thence by a direct line to the Sink Hole springs, thence by a line north sixty degrees East until it intersects a north line running from the Great Cave on the Ohio river, and the alterations and boundaries so established shall take place from and after the first day of May next.

[Executive Journal of Indiana Territory, page 117.]

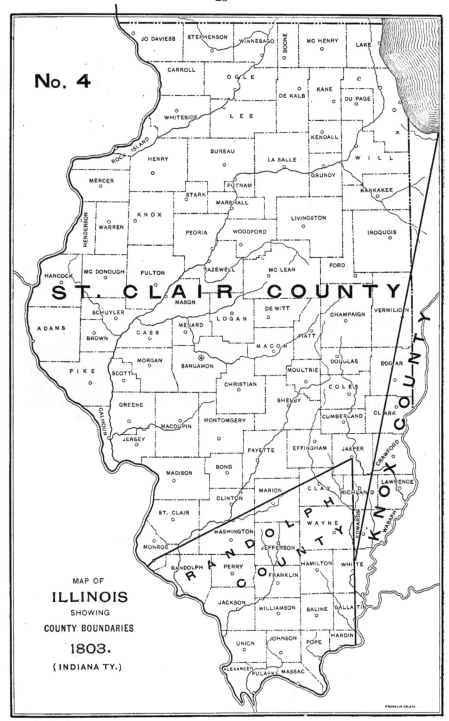

No. 4

ST. CLAIR COUNTY

MAP OF
ILLINOIS
SHOWING
COUNTY BOUNDARIES
1803.
(INDIANA TY.)

1809—ST. CLAIR AND RANDOLPH.

As counties of Illinois Territory.

A PROCLAMATION BY NATHANIEL POPE, SECRETARY OF THE TERRITORY OF
ILLINOIS AND EXERCISING THE GOVERNMENT THEREOF.

By virtue of the powers vested in the Governor for the prevention of crimes and injuries and for the execution of process civil and criminal within the Territory; I have thought proper to, and by this proclamation do, divide the Illinois Territory into two counties to be called the COUNTY OF ST. CLAIR and the COUNTY OF RANDOLPH. The county of Randolph shall include all that part of the Illinois Territory lying south of the line dividing the counties of Randolph and St. Clair as it existed under the government of the Indiana Territory on the last day of February in the year one thousand eight hundred and nine. And the County of St. Clair shall include all that part of the Territory which lies north of said line.
Done at Kaskaskia, the 28th day of April, 1809, and of the Independence of the United States the thirty-third.

NAT. POPE.

[Territorial Records of Illinois, p. 3.]

No. 5

MAP OF
ILLINOIS
SHOWING
COUNTY BOUNDARIES
1809.
(ILLINOIS TY.)

1812—MADISON, GALLATIN AND JOHNSON.

As counties of Illinois Territory.

A PROCLAMATION.

By virtue of the powers vested in the Governor of the Territory, I do hereby lay off a county or district to be called the COUNTY OF MADISON to be included within the following bounds, viz.: To begin on the Mississippi, to run with the second township line above Cahokia east until it strikes the dividing line between the Illinois and Indiana Territories; thence with said dividing line to the line of Upper Canada; thence with said line to the Mississippi; and thence down the Mississippi to the beginning. I do appoint the house of Thomas Kirkpatrick to be the seat of justice of said county.

I do also lay off a county or district to be called the COUNTY OF GALLATIN, to be bounded as follows, viz.: To begin at the mouth of Lusk's Creek on the Ohio, running up with said creek to Miles' Trace; thence along said trace to Big Muddy; thence up Big Muddy to its source; thence north to the line of St. Clair County; thence with said line to the Wabash; thence down the Wabash and Ohio, to the beginning. And I do appoint Shawnee Town to be the seat of justice of Gallatin County.

And I do lay off a county or district to be called JOHNSON COUNTY to be bounded as follows, viz.: To begin at the mouth of Lusk's Creek on the Ohio; thence with the line of Gallatin county to Big Muddy; thence down Big Muddy and the Mississippi to the mouth of the Ohio, and up the Ohio to the beginning. And I do appoint the house of John Bradshaw to be the seat of justice for Johnson County.

Done at Kaskaskia the 14th day of September, 1812, and the Independence of the United States the thirty-seventh.

By the Governor: NINIAN EDWARDS.

NAT. POPE, Secretary.

[Territorial Records of Illinois, page 26.[

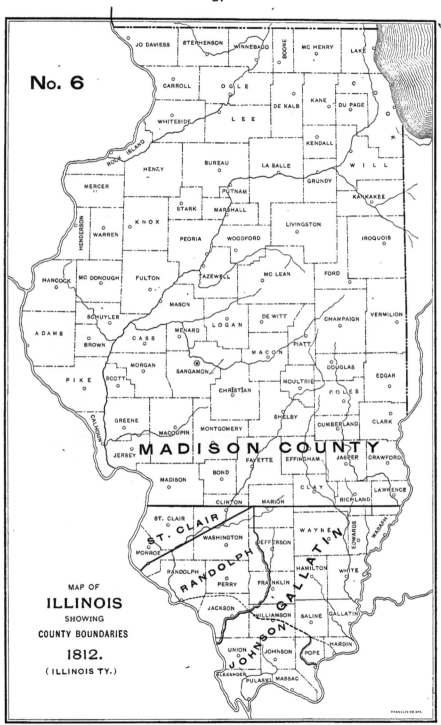

No. 6

MAP OF
ILLINOIS
SHOWING
COUNTY BOUNDARIES
1812.
(ILLINOIS TY.)

1813 COUNTY BOUNDARIES RE-ADJUSTED.

By Territorial Legislature.

An Act Establishing the Boundary Lines of Gallatin County.

Be it enacted by the Legislative Council and House of Representatives of the Illinois Territory, and it is hereby enacted by the authority of the same: That the line of Gallatin County do begin at the mouth of Lusk's creek on the Ohio river, running up with said creek to Miles' old Trace; thence along said Trace to the meridian line which runs north from the mouth of the Ohio river; thence north with said line to the lower line of Madison county; thence with said line to the dividing line between Illinois and Indiana Territories; thence with said line to the mouth of the Wabash, and thence down the Ohio to the beginning.
Approved Dec. 11, 1813.

An Act Establishing the Boundary Line Between the Counties of Randolph and St. Clair.

Be it enacted by the Legislative Council and House of Representatives of the Illinois Territory and it is hereby enacted by the authority of the same: That the boundary line between St. Clair, Randolph and Gallatin counties shall begin at the Mississippi river on the line between townships 3 and 4 south of the base line (which is near Cahokia); thence running east along said line between townships 3 and 4 aforesaid to the meridian line which runs north from the mouth of the Ohio river; thence along said meridian line until it intersects the lower (or southern) boundary of the county of Madison. This act to be in force from and after its passage.
Approved Dec. 11, 1813.
[Territorial Laws 1813; Manuscript Nos. 428, 429; unpublished.]

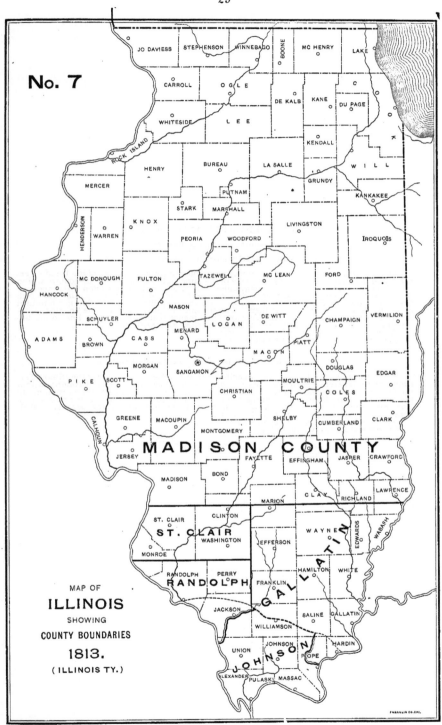

No. 7

MAP OF
ILLINOIS
SHOWING
COUNTY BOUNDARIES
1813.
(ILLINOIS TY.)

1814-15—EDWARDS AND WHITE.

As counties of Illinois Territory.

AN ACT FOR THE DIVISION OF GALLATIN COUNTY.

Be it enacted by the Legislative Council and House of Representatives of the Illinois Ter ritory and it is hereby enacted by authority of the same. That all that tract of country within the following boundaries (to wit): Beginning at the mouth of Bompast [Bon Pas] creek on the Big Wabash, and running thence due west to the meridian line which runs due north from the mouth of the Ohio river; thence with said meridian line and due north until it strikes the line of Upper Canada; thence with the line of Upper Canada to the line that separates this Territory from the Indiana Territory; and thence with said dividing line to the be ginning shall constitute a seperate county, to be called EDWARDS.

Approved this 28th day of November, 1814.

[Territorial Laws, 1814, Pope's Digest, p. 85.]

AN ACT FOR THE DIVISION OF GALLATIN COUNTY.

Be it enacted by the Legislative Council and House of Representatives of the Illinois Territory, and it is hereby enacted by authority of the same, That all that tract of country within the following boundaries (to wit): Beginning at the mouth of the Little Wabash, running up the same to Joseph Boon's mill; thence due west to the third principal meridian; thence with Edwards county line east to the Big Wabash, thence down the same to the beginning shall constitute a separate county, to be called WHITE

Approved this 9th day of December, 1815.

[Territorial Laws, 1815-16, p. 5.]

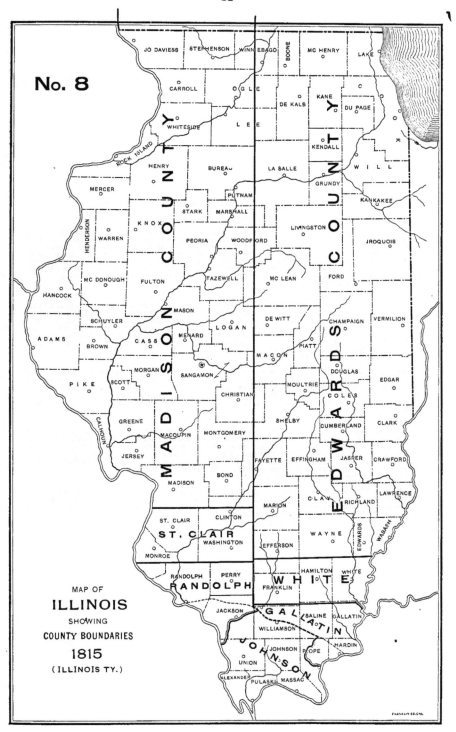

No. 8

MAP OF
ILLINOIS
SHOWING
COUNTY BOUNDARIES
1815
(ILLINOIS TY.)

1816—JACKSON, POPE, MONROE AND CRAWFORD.

As counties of Illinois Territory.

MONROE. Jan. 6—Beginning on the Mississippi river where the base line, which is about three-fourths of a mile below Judge Biggs's present residence, strikes the said river; thence with the base line until it strikes the first township line therefrom; thence southeast to the southeast corner of township two south, range nine west; thence south to the southeast corner of township four north, range nine west; thence south-westwardly to the Mississippi, so as to include Alexander McNabb's farm, and thence up the Mississippi to the beginning shall constitute a separate county, to be called MONROE.
[Territorial Laws, 1815-16, p. 25.]

JACKSON. Jan. 10—Beginning at the mouth of the Big Muddy river and running up the same to the township line between ten and eleven; thence east with said line to the principal meridian line running from the mouth of the Ohio river; thence north with the meridian line thirty miles; thence west twenty-four miles to the corner of range between four and five west of the principal meridian line; thence south six miles to the township corner between six and seven; thence to the headwaters of the creek called Gagnic and down it to the Mississippi; thence down the Mississippi to the beginning shall be a separate and distinct county and called and be known by the name of JACKSON.
[Territorial Laws, 1815-16, p. 62.]

POPE. Jan. 10—Beginning on the Ohio river where the meridian line leaves it that divides ranges number three and four east of the third principal meridian; thence north to the township line dividing townships ten and eleven south; thence east eighteen miles; thence to that point on the Ohio where the line dividing ranges eight and nine leaves it; thence down the same to the beginning shall constitute a separate county, to be called and known by the name of POPE.
[Territorial Laws, 1815-16, p. 66.]*.

CRAWFORD. Dec. 31—Beginning at the mouth of the Embarras and running with said river to the intersection of the line dividing townships number three and four north, of range eleven west, of the second principal meridian; thence west with said township line to the meridian and due north until it strikes the line of Upper Canada; thence to the line that separates this territory from the state of Indiana; and thence south with said dividing line to the beginning shall constitute a separate county, to be called CRAWFORD.
[Territorial Laws, 1816-17, p. 21.]

*NOTE—The northeastern line of Pope county was changed by act of Dec. 26, 1816, and established as follows: ."Beginning at Rock and Cave [Cave-in-Rock] on the Ohio river; thence a straight line to the corner of townships number ten and eleven south and ranges number seven and eight, east of the third principal meridian."
[Territorial Laws, 1816-17, p. 10.]

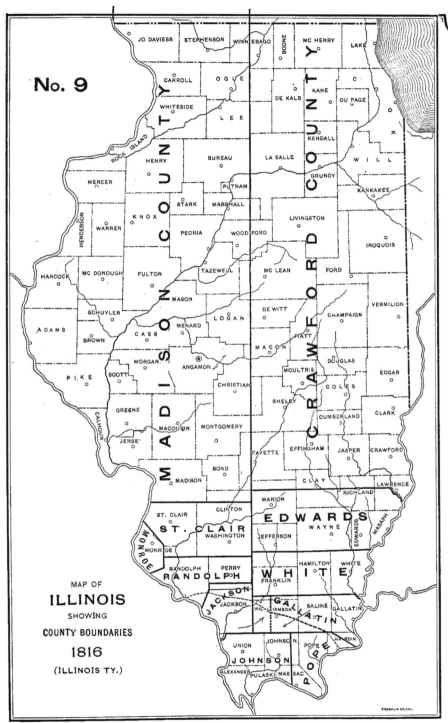

No. 9

MAP OF
ILLINOIS
SHOWING
COUNTY BOUNDARIES
1816
(ILLINOIS TY.)

1817—BOND.

As a county of Illinois Territory.

BOND. Jan 4—Beginning at the southwest corner of township number three north of range four west; thence east to the southeast [west] corner of township number three north of range number one east, to the the third principal meridian line; thence north to the boundary line of the territory; thence west with said boundary line so far that a south line will pass between ranges four and five west; thence south with said line to the beginning, shall constitute a separate county to be called BOND. ·

[Territorial Laws, 1816-17, p. 28.]

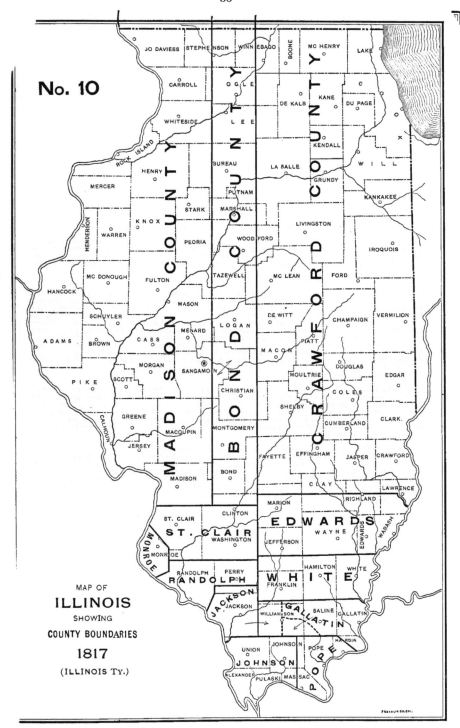

No. 10

MAP OF
ILLINOIS
SHOWING
COUNTY BOUNDARIES
1817
(ILLINOIS Ty.)

1818—FRANKLIN, UNION AND WASHINGTON.

As counties of Illinois Territory.

FRANKLIN. Jan. 2—Beginning at the corner of township ten and eleven on the line between ranges four and five [east]; thence north with said line thirty-six miles; thence west twenty-four miles to the third principal meridian;thence south with the same to the line divid ing townships ten and eleven; thence east to the beginning, shall constitute a separate county to be called FRANKLIN.
[Territorial Laws, 1817-18, p. 11.]

UNION. Jan. 2—Beginning on the range line between ranges one and two east, at corner of townships ten and eleven south; thence south along the said range line eighteen miles to the corner of townships thirteen and fourteen south; thence west along the township line between townships thirteen and fourteen south to the Mississippi river; thence up the Mississippi river to the mouth of the Big Muddy river; thence up the Big Muddy river to where the township line between townships ten and eleven south crosses the same; thence east along the said township line to the beginning shall constitute a separate county to be called UNION COUNTY: Provided, however, that all that tract of country lying south of township thirteen south, to the Ohio and Mississippi rivers, and west of the range line between ranges one and two east shall, until the same be formed into a separate county, be attached to and be a part of Union County.
[Territorial Laws, 1817-18, p. 15.]

WASHINGTON. Jan 2—Commencing at the north west corner of township number two north, range number five west; thence east to the north east [corner] of township number two north on the third principal meridian line; thence south with the said meridian line to the southeast corner of township number three south; thence west to the southwest corner of township three south, of range five west; thence north between ranges five and six west, to the beginning, shall constitute a separate and distinct county to be called WASHINGTON.
[Territorial Laws, 1817-18, p. 39.]

JOHNSON. Jan. 2—Boundaries re-defined. Beginning on the range line between ranges four and five east of the third principal meridian at the corner between townships ten and eleven south of the base line; thence south along the said range line to the Ohio river; thence down along the Ohio river to where the range line between ranges one and two east intersects said river; thence north along the said range line to the corner of townships ten and eleven south to the beginning. And all that part of Pope County which is included within this boundary shall here after be attached to and form a part of JOHNSON COUNTY.
[Territorial Laws, 1817-18, p. 15.]

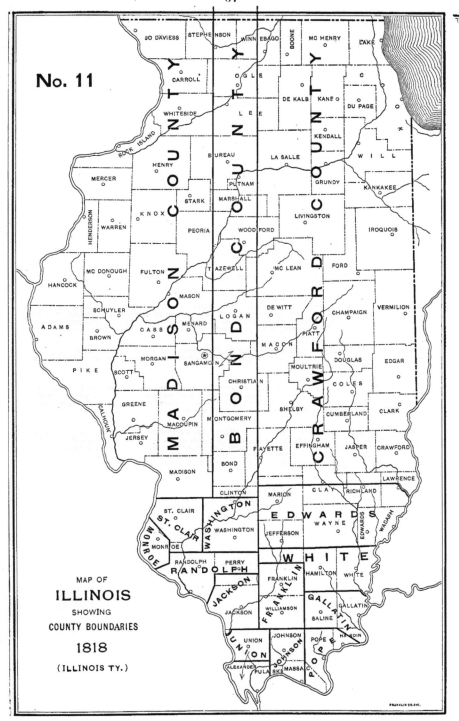

No. 11

MAP OF
ILLINOIS
SHOWING
COUNTY BOUNDARIES
1818
(ILLINOIS TY.)

1819—ALEXANDER, CLARK, JEFFERSON AND WAYNE.

As counties of the State of Illinois.

ALEXANDER. March 4—All that tract of country within the following boundaries, to-wit: West of the line between ranges 1 and 2 east of the third principal meridian and south of the line between townships 13 and 14 south of the base line to the boundaries of this State on the Ohio and Mississippi, shall constitute a county to be called ALEXANDER.
[Laws 1819, p. 113.]

CLARK. March 22—All that part of Crawford county lying north of a line beginning on the Great Wabash river dividing townships 8 and 9 north, running due west, shall form a new and separate county to be called CLARK.
[Laws 1819, p. 166.]

JEFFERSON. March 26—Beginning where the line between ranges 4 and 5 east intersects the base line; thence west with said line to the third principal meridian; thence south twenty-four miles; thence east twenty-four miles; thence north to the place of beginning, shall constitute a separate county to be called JEFFERSON.
[Laws 1819, p. 267.]

WAYNE. March 26—Beginning on the White county line on the line dividing ranges 9 and 10 east of the third principal meridian; thence north to the line dividing townships 3 and 4, to the Crawford county line, north of the base line; thence west to the line dividing ranges 4 and 5 east of the third principal meridian line; thence south to the White county line; thence east to the beginning, shall constitute a separate county to be called WAYNE.
[Laws 1819, p. 268.]

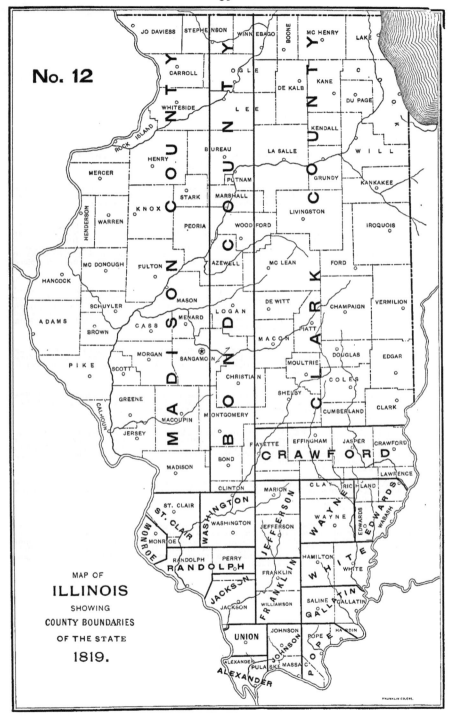

No. 12

MAP OF
ILLINOIS
SHOWING
COUNTY BOUNDARIES
OF THE STATE
1819.

1821—LAWRENCE, GREENE, SANGAMON, PIKE, HAMILTON, MONTGOMERY AND FAYETTE.

LAWRENCE. Jan. 16.—Beginning on the Great Wabash seven miles north of the base line, thence west to the Wayne county line; thence north two miles north of town 4; thence east to the Wabash; thence with that river to the place of beginning.
[Laws 1821, p. 16.]

GREENE. Jan. 20.—Beginning at the southeast corner town 7 north, 10 west of third principal meridian; thence north between ranges 9 and 10 to the northeast corner of town 12 north; thence west along the line between towns 12 and 13 to the middle of the Illinois; thence down said river to the Mississippi; thence down the middle of the river to a point parallel with the southwest corner of town 6 north, 10 west; thence north with the range line between 10 and 11, to the township line between 6 and 7; thence east with said township line to the place of beginning.
[Laws 1821, p. 26.]

SANGAMON. Jan. 30.—From the northeast corner of town 12 north, 1 west of third principal meridian, north with that meridian to the Illinois river; down the middle of the river to the mouth of Balance or Negro (Indian) creek; up said creek to its head; thence through the middle of the prairie dividing the waters of the Sangamon and Mauvaise Terre to the northwest corner of town 12 north, 7 west of the third principal meridian; thence east along the north line of town 12 to the place of beginning.
[Laws 1821, p. 45.]

PIKE. January 31.—Up the middle of the Illinois river from its mouth to the fork; up the south fork (Kankakee) to the Indiana state line; north with the state line to the north boundary of the State; west with said State line to the west boundary of the State; thence with said boundary to the place of beginning.
[Laws 1821, p. 59.]

HAMILTON. Feb. 8.—South from the southern line of Wayne county, on the line dividing ranges 7 and 8 east, to Gallatin county; thence west eighteen miles to Franklin; thence north to the Wayne county line; thence east to the beginning.
[Laws 1821, p. 113.]

MONTGOMERY. Feb. 12.—West from the southeast corner of section 24, town 7 north, 2 west, to the southwest corner section 19, town 7 north, 4 west; thence south to southeast corner of town 7 north, 5 west; thence west to southwest corner of said township; thence north to northwest corner of town 12 north, 5 west; thence east to northeast corner of town 12 north, 2 west; thence south to the beginning
[Laws 1821, p. 142.]

FAYETTE. Feb. 14.—All that tract of country lying north of a line running east from the southwest corner of town 3 north, 1 west, to the southeast corner of town 3 north, 6 east of the third principal meridian.*
[Laws 1821, p. 164.]

---

*NOTE.—A strict construction of this act would make the entire western boundary of Fayette county the line between ranges one and two west, and extend its northern boundary to the Wisconsin line, thus taking one range of townships from the east side of Sangamon (formed Jan. 30) and cutting Pike (formed Jan. 31) in two. It is probable that the word "unorganized" should be read into the act so as to make it read "all that tract of *unorganized* country lying north" etc. Subsequent acts seem to justify this theory.

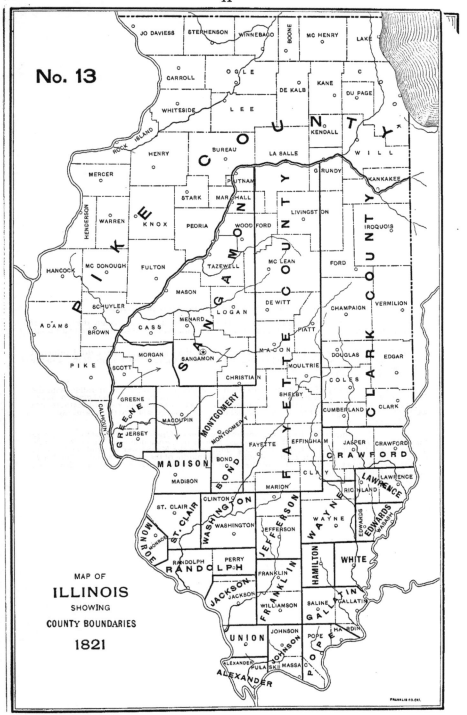

No. 13

MAP OF
ILLINOIS
SHOWING
COUNTY BOUNDARIES
1821

1823 EDGAR, MARION, FULTON AND MORGAN.

EDGAR. January 3—From the Indiana State line west 24 miles through the center of township 12 north; thence north 27 miles; thence east 24 miles; thence south to the beginning.
[Laws 1823, p. 74.]

MARION. January 24—From the intersection of the base line with the third principal meridian, north along said meridian 24 miles; thence east 24 miles; thence south 24 miles to the base line; thence west to the beginning.
[Laws 1823, p. 49.]

FULTON. January 28—From the intersection of the fourth principal meridian with the Illinois river; thence up the middle of the river till intersected by the range line between ranges 5 and 6 east; thence north with said range line to the line between towns 9 and 10 north; thence west with said town line to the fourth principal meridian, thence south to the beginning.
[Laws 1823, p. 88.]

MORGAN. January 31—From the northwest corner of Greene county, east to the range line between 7 and 8 west of the third principal meridian; thence northerly along the middle of the prairie dividing the waters of the Sangamon from the Mauvaisterre, Apple and Indian creeks, to the middle of range 8; thence north to the middle of the main channel of the Sangamon; thence down to the middle of the main channel of the Illinois; thence down the Illinois to the beginning.
[Laws 1823, p. 108.]

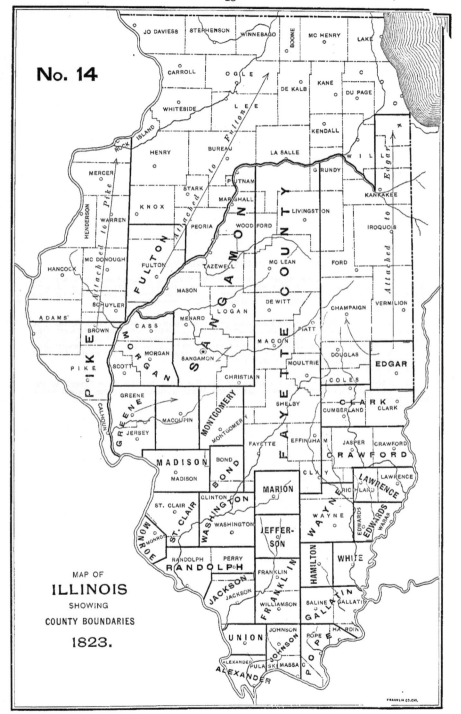

No. 14

MAP OF
ILLINOIS
SHOWING
COUNTY BOUNDARIES
1823.

1824—CLAY, CLINTON AND WABASH.

CLAY. Dec. 23—From the intersection of the line dividing ranges 4 and 5 east with the middle line of town 2 north; thence east with said line to the Fox river; thence north with said river to the line dividing towns 5 and 6 north; thence west with said line to the range line dividing 4 and 5 east; thence south with said range line to the beginning.
[Laws 1825, p. 19.]

CLINTON. Dec. 27—Down the Kaskaskia from the mouth of Crooked creek to the line dividing St. Clair and Washington; thence north on the range line between 5 and 6 west to the northwest corner of town 2 north, 5 west; thence east to the southeast corner of town 3 north, 5 west; thence north to the northwest corner of town 3 north, 4 west; thence east twenty-four miles; thence south along the third principal meridian sixteen miles; thence west to Crooked creek; thence down said creek to the beginning.
[Laws of 1825, p. 27.]

WABASH. Dec. 27—From the mouth of De Bon Pas creek up the main branch to the south line of Lawrence county; thence east to the Wabash; thence down the Wabash to the place of beginning.
[Laws 1825, p. 25.]

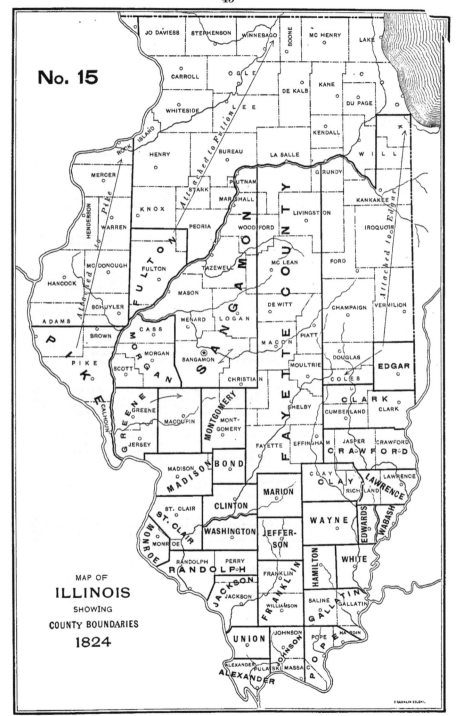

No. 15

MAP OF
ILLINOIS
SHOWING
COUNTY BOUNDARIES
1824

46

1825—TEN NEW COUNTIES.

CALHOUN. Jan. 10—All that tract of country between the Illinois and Mississippi rivers south of the line between townships 7 and 8 south.
[Laws 1825, p. 65.]

ADAMS. Jan. 13—From the southeast corner town 3 south, 5 west of the fourth principal meridian, west to the Mississippi; thence up the river to the line between towns 2 and 3 north; thence east to the northeast corner of town 2 north, 5 west; thence south to the beginning.
[Laws 1825, p. 93.]

HANCOCK. Jan. 13—East from the Mississippi on the line between towns 2 and 3 north, to the line between ranges 4 and 5 west, of the fourth principal meridian; thence north to the line between towns 7 and 8 north; thence west to the Mississippi; thence down the river to the beginning.
[Laws 1825, p. 93.]

HENRY. Jan. 13—East from the fourth principal meridian on the line between towns 12 and 13 north, to the line between ranges 4 and 5 east; thence north to the Wisconsin state line; thence west to the fourth principal meridian; thence south to the beginning.
[Laws 1825, p. 94.]

KNOX. Jan. 13—East from the fourth principal meridian on the line between towns 8 and 9 north, to the line between ranges 4 and 5 east; thence north to the line between towns 12 and 13 north; thence west to the fourth principal meridian; thence south to the beginning.
[Laws 1825, p. 94.]

MERCER. Jan. 13—East from the Mississippi on the line between towns 12 and 13 north, to the fourth principal meridian; thence north to the Wisconsin state line; thence west to the Mississippi; thence down the river to the beginning.
[Laws 1825, p. 93.]

PEORIA. Jan. 13—West from the Illinois on the line between towns 11 and 12 north, to the line between ranges 4 and 5 east; thence south to the line between towns 7 and 8 north; thence east to the line between ranges 5 and 6 east; thence south to the Illinois; thence up the river to the beginning.
[Laws 1825, p. 85.]

PUTNAM. Jan. 13—Up the Illinois from the line between towns 11 and 12 north, to the south fork [Kankakee]; thence up said fork to the Indiana state line; thence north along said line to the northeast corner of the State; thence west to the line between ranges 4 and 5 east; thence south to the line between towns 11 and 12 north; thence east to the beginning.
[Laws 1825, p. 94.]

SCHUYLER. Jan. 13—West from the Illinois on the line between towns 2 and 3 south, to the line between ranges 4 and 5 west; thence north to the line between towns 3 and 4 north; thence east to the fourth principal meridian; thence south to the line between towns 2 and 3 north; thence east to the Illinois; thence down the river to the beginning.
[Laws 1825, p. 92.]

WARREN. Jan. 13—East from the Mississippi on the line between towns 7 and 8 north, to the fourth principal meridian; thence north to the line between towns 12 and 13 north; thence west to the Mississippi; thence down the river to the beginning.
[Laws 1825, p. 93.]

SANGAMON. Dec. 23—Boundary re-defined, decreasing area. North from the southeast corner of town 13 north, 1 west, to the north line of town 20; thence west to the middle of the Illinois; thence down to the mouth of the Sangamon; thence up the Sangamon to the middle of range 8 west; thence south with the east line of Morgan to the south line of town 13 north; thence east to the beginning
[Laws 1825, p. 20.]

MADISON. Jan. 3—Territory added.
[Laws 1825, p. 53.]

MONROE. Jan. 15—Territory added.
[Laws 1825, p. 109. Also Jan. 9, Private laws 1827, p. 8, and Jan. 20, Laws 1829, p. 31.]

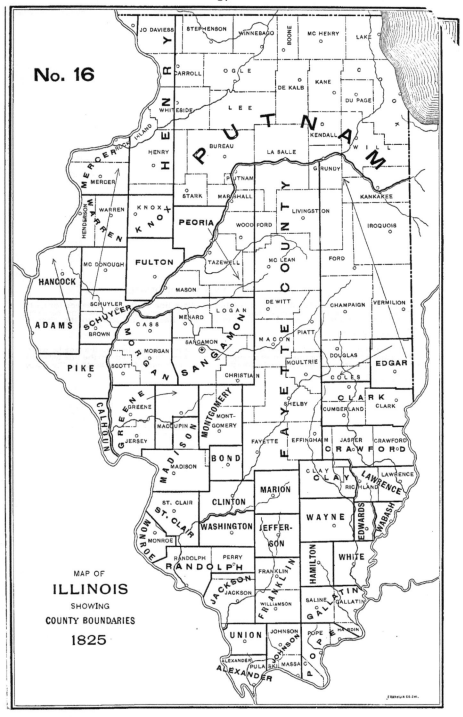

No. 16

MAP OF
ILLINOIS
SHOWING
COUNTY BOUNDARIES
1825

1826 VERMILION AND McDONOUGH.

VERMILION. Jan. 18—West from the Indiana state line on the line between towns 16 and 17 north, to the line between ranges 9 and 10 east; thence north to the line between towns 22 and 23 north; thence east to the Indiana state line; thence south to the place of beginning.
[Laws 1826, p. 50.]

McDONOUGH. Jan. 25—West from the fourth principal meridian on the line between towns 7 and 8 north, to the line between ranges 4 and 5 west; thence south to the line between towns 3 and 4 north; thence east to the fourth principal meridian; thence north to the place of beginning.
[Laws 1826, p. 76.]

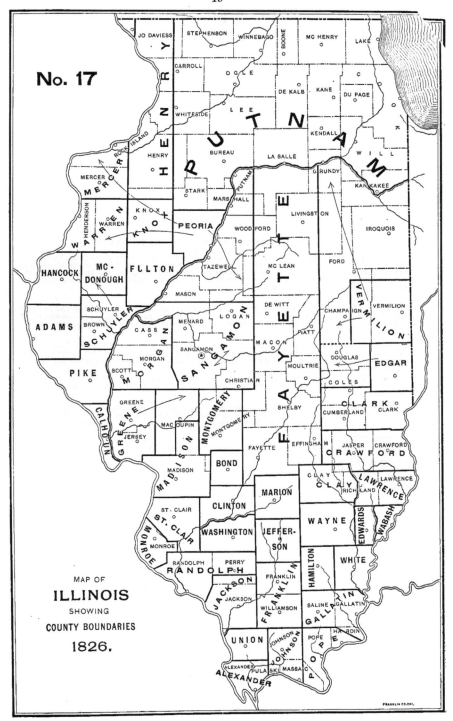

No. 17

MAP OF
ILLINOIS
SHOWING
COUNTY BOUNDARIES
1826.

1827—SHELBY, PERRY, TAZEWELL AND JO DAVIESS.

SHELBY. Jan. 23—North thirty miles from the northwest corner of section 19, town 9 north, 1 east of the third principal meridian to the northwest corner of section 19, town 14 north, 1 east; thence east thirty-six miles to the northeast corner of section 24, town 14 north, 6 east; thence south thirty miles to the southeast corner of section 13, town 9 north, 6 east; thence west thirty-six miles to the place of beginning.
[Laws 1827, p. 115.]

PERRY. Jan. 29—West from the third principal meridian on the line between towns 3 and south to line between ranges 4 and 5 west; thence south to the line between towns 6 and 7 south; thence east to the third principal meridian; thence north to the place of beginning.
[Laws 1827, p. 110.]

TAZEWELL. Jan. 31—North from the northeast corner of town 20 north, [3] east of the third principal meridian to the line between towns 28 and 29 north; thence west to the Illinois; thence down the river to the line between towns 20 and 21 north; thence east to the beginning.
[Laws 1827, p. 113.]
NOTE—This act does not clearly indicate the place of beginning, but the act of Jan. 22, 1829, fixes the initial point at the northeast corner of town 20 north, 3 east of the third principal meridian.

JO DAVIESS. Feb. 17—From the northwest corner of the State down the Mississippi to the northern line of the Military Tract [the line between towns 15 and 16 north]; thence east to the Illinois; thence north to the Wisconsin state line; thence west to the place of beginning.
[Laws 1827, p. 117.]
NOTE—By this act Putnam was divided into two distinct tracts.

MONROE. Jan. 15—Territory added. East line carried to the Kaskaskia.
[Private Laws 1827, p. 8.]

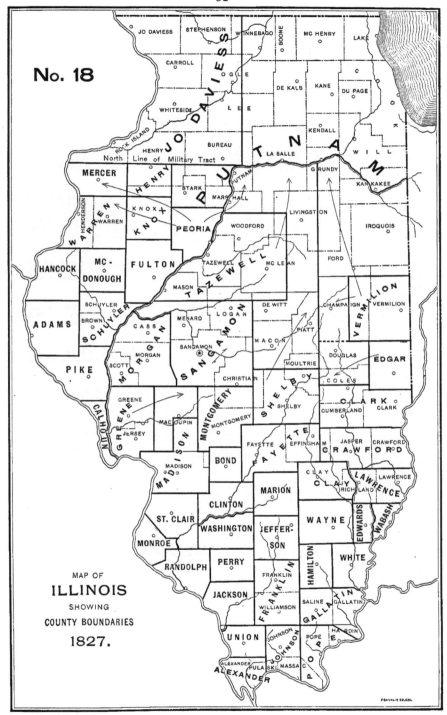

No. 18

MAP OF
ILLINOIS
SHOWING
COUNTY BOUNDARIES
1827.

1829-1831—NINE NEW COUNTIES.

MACOUPIN. Jan. 17, 1829—East from the southwest corner of town 7 north, 9 west, to the southwest corner of Montgomery: thence north to the south line of Sangamon; thence west to the line between ranges 9 and 10 west; thence south to the beginning.
[Laws 1829, p. 26.]

MACON. Jan. 19, 1829—North on the third principal meridian from the southwest corner of section 18, town 14 north, 1 east, to the line between towns 20 and 21 north; thence east to the line dividing ranges 6 and 7 east; thence south to the southeast corner of section 13, town 14 north, 6 east; thence west to the beginning.
[Laws 1829, p. 28.]

COLES. Dec. 25, 1830—West from the northeast corner of section 4, town 16 north, 14 west, of second principal meridian to the line between ranges 6 and 7 east of the third principal meridian; thence south to the southeast corner of town 9 north, 6 east, thence east to the southeast corner of section 31 (the east line of fractional range 11 east); thence north to the northeast corner of section 19, town 12 north, 11 east of the third principal meridian; thence east to the north east corner of section 21, town 12 north, 14 west of the second principal meridian; thence north on the section lines through the middle of range 14 west to the beginning.
[Laws 1831, p. 59.]

McLEAN. Dec 25, 1830—North from the southwest corner of town 21 north, 1 west, of the third principal meridian to the line dividing towns 28 and 29 north; thence east to the line dividing ranges 6 and 7 east; thence south to the southeast corner of town 21 north, 6 east; thence west to the beginning.
[Laws 1831, p. 31.]

COOK. Jan. 15, 1831—West from the Indiana state line on the line dividing towns 33 and 34 north to the line dividing ranges 8 and 9 east of the third principal meridian; thence north to the Wisconsin state line; thence east to the northeast corner of the state; thence southwardly along the state line to the beginning
[Laws 1831, p. 54.]

LA SALLE. Jan 15, 1831—South from the southwest corner of Cook 30 miles; thence west to the third principal meridian; thence north 48 miles; thence east to Cook; thence south to the beginning.
[Laws 1831, p. 54.]

PUTNAM (re-defined). Jan. 15, 1831—East from the southwest corner of town 12 north, 6 east to the Illinois; thence down the river to the south line of town 29 north; thence east to the third principal meridian; thence north 22 miles; thence west to the northwest corner of town 18 north, 6 east of the fourth principal meridian; thence south to the beginning.
[Laws 1831, p. 54.]

ROCK ISLAND. Feb. 9, 1831—East from middle of the main channel of the Mississippi with the north line of town 15 north to the fourth principal meridian; thence north to Rock river; thence up the middle of the main channel to its confluence with Marais d'ogee slough; thence with the middle of said slough to the Mississippi; thence down the middle of the main channel of the river to the beginning.
[Laws 1831, p. 52.]

EFFINGHAM. Feb. 15, 1831—South from the northwest corner of Jasper to the line between towns 5 and 6 north; thence west to the line between ranges 3 and 4 east of the third principal meridian; thence north to the northwest corner of section 19, town 9 north, 4 east; thence east to the northeast corner of section 24, town 9 north, 6 east; thence south to the south east corner of town 9 north, 6 east; thence east to the line between ranges 7 and 8 east; thence south to the beginning.
[Laws 1831, p. 51.]

JASPER. Feb 15, 1831—North with section lines from the southeast corner of section 22, town 5 north, 14 west of the second principal meridian to the north east corner of section 3 town 8 north, 14 west; thence west to the northwest corner of section 6, town 8 north, 8 east of third principal meridian; thence south to the southwest corner of section 19, town 5 north, 8 east; thence east to the beginning.
[Laws 1831, p. 51.]

MONROE. Jan. 20—Southern boundary re-adjusted.
[Laws 1829, p. 31.]

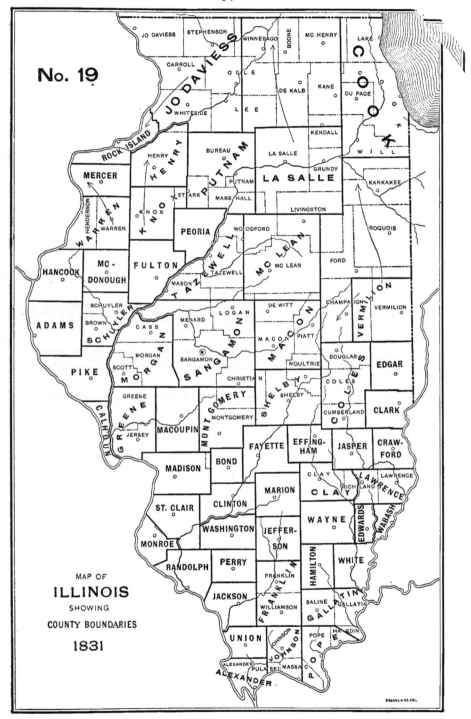

No. 19

MAP OF
ILLINOIS
SHOWING
COUNTY BOUNDARIES
1831

1833 1835—CHAMPAIGN AND IROQUOIS.

CHAMPAIGN. Feb. 20, 1833—West from the southwest corner of section 34, town 16 north, 14 west of the second principal meridian to the east line of Macon; thence north to the line between towns 22 and 23 north; thence east to the northwest corner of section 3, town 22 north, 14 west; thence south on section lines to the beginning.
[Private laws 1833, p. 28.]:

IROQUOIS. Feb. 26, 1833—West from the Indiana state line along the line between towns 23 and 24 north, to the line between ranges 9 and 10 east of the third principal meridian; thence north to the south line of Cook; thence east to the Indiana state line; thence south to the beginning.
[Private laws 1833, p. 19.]

VERMILION. Feb. 26, 1833—Territory added—All that tract lying between the northern boundary of Vermilion and the southern boundary of Iroquois, added to Vermilion.
[Private laws 1833, p. 20.]

PERRY AND FRANKLIN. Feb. 6, 1835—Boundary between re-defined. The Little Muddy declared the boundary line.
[Laws 1835, p. 36.]

MORGAN AND SANGAMON. Feb. 12, 1835—Boundary between re-defined, and provision made for survey thereof.
[Laws 1835, p. 62.]

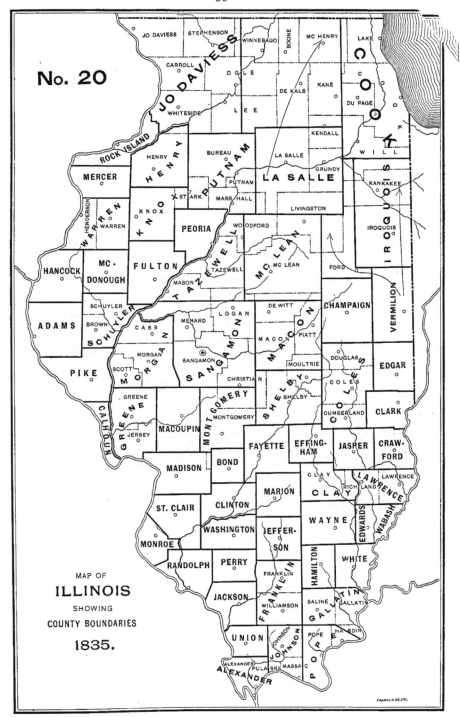

No. 20

MAP OF
ILLINOIS
SHOWING
COUNTY BOUNDARIES
1835.

1836—SIX NEW COUNTIES.

WILL. Jan. 12.—East from the northwest corner of town 37 north, range 9 east, to the east line of range 10 east; thence south six miles; thence east six miles; thence south six miles; thence east six miles; thence south six miles; thence east to the Indiana state line; thence south to the Kankakee; thence down the same to the north line of town 31 north; thence west to the west line of range 9 east; thence north to the beginning.
[Laws 1836, p. 262.]

KANE. Jan. 16.—South from the northeast corner of town 42 north, 8 east, to the southeast corner of town 37 north, 8 east; thence west to the southeast corner of town 37 north, 2 east; thence north to the north line of town 42; thence east to beginning.
[Laws 1836, p. 273.]

McHENRY. Jan. 16.—West from Lake Michigan on line between towns 42 and 43 north to the east line of range 4 east; thence north to the Wisconsin state line; thence east to Lake Michigan; thence with the shore of said lake to the beginning.
[Laws 1836, p. 273.]

OGLE. Jan. 16.—North from the southwest corner of town 19 north, 8 east of the fourth principal meridian, to the southwest corner of town 26 north, 8 east; thence east to the third principal meridian; thence south to the southwest corner of town 43 north, 1 east of the third principal meridian; thence east to the southeast corner of town 43 north, 2 east; thence south to the southeast corner of town 37 north, 2 east; thence west to the third principal meridian; thence south to the southeast corner of town 19 north, 11 east of the fourth principal meridian; thence west to the beginning.
[Laws 1836, p. 274.]

WHITESIDE. Jan. 16.—West from the southeast corner of town 19 north, 7 east of the fourth principal meridian, to Rock river; thence down the middle of the river to the Meredocia (Marais d'ogee slough); thence with the middle of the Meredocia to the Mississippi; thence up the middle of the main channel of the river to the north line of town 22 north; thence east to the southeast corner of town 23 north, 7 east; thence south to the beginning.
[Laws 1836, p. 274.]

WINNEBAGO. Jan. 16.—West from the southeast corner of town 43 north, 4 east of the third principal meridian, to the third principal meridian; thence north to the southeast corner of town 26 north, 11 east of the fourth principal meridian; thence west to the west line of range 8 east of the fourth principal meridian; thence north to the Wisconsin state line; thence east to the northeast corner of range 4 east of the third principal meridian; thence south to the beginning.
[Laws 1836, p. 273.]

JO DAVIESS. Jan. 16.—Boundaries re-defined.—East from the Mississippi along the north line of town 22 north to the west line of range 8 east of the fourth principal meridian; thence north to the Wisconsin state line; thence west to the Mississippi; thence down the river to the beginning.
[Laws 1836, p. 273.]

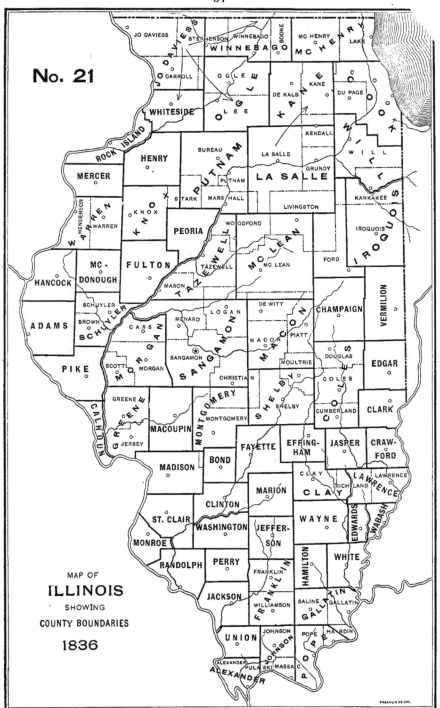

No. 21

MAP OF
ILLINOIS
SHOWING
COUNTY BOUNDARIES
1836

1837-1839—TWENTY ONE NEW COUNTIES.

1837.

Livingston............................Established Feb. 27.......Laws 1837, page....... 83
Bureau................................Established Feb. 28......Laws 1837, page 93
Cass ....Established Mar. 3......Laws 1837, page....... 101
Boone.................................Established Mar. 4......Laws 1837, page....... 96
DeKalb................................Established Mar. 4......Laws 1837, page....... 97
Stephenson............................Established Mar. 4......Laws 1837, page....... 96

Winnebago, boundary re-defined..............,..... Mar. 4.......Laws 1837, page....... 96
McHenry, eastern boundary defined............... Mar. 4......Laws 1837, page....... 89
Henry, territory detached.................... Mar. 4......Laws 1837, page....... 89
Adams, Hancock, Warren and Mercer, western boundary defined, Mar. 4, Laws 1837, page 91

1839.

Marshall..............................Established Jan. 19.......Laws 1839, page....... 43
Brown ....Established Feb. 1.......Laws 1839, page....... 52
DuPage ....Established Feb. 9......Laws 1839, page....... 73
Dane (now Christian)..................Established Feb. 15......Laws 1839, page....... 104
Logan.................................Established Feb. 15......Laws 1839, page....... 104
Menard ....Established Fen. 15......Laws 1839, page....... 104
Scott ....Established Feb. 16......Laws 1839, page....... 126
Carroll................................Established Feb. 22......Laws 1839, page....... 160
Lee....................................Established Feb. 27......Laws 1839, page....... 170
Jersey.................................Established Feb. 28......Laws 1839, page....... 208
Warren................................Established Feb. 28......Laws 1839, page....... 110
DeWitt................................Established Mar. 1......Laws 1839, page....... 199
Lake.................................. ....Established Mar. 1......Laws 1839, page....... 216
Hardin ....Established Mar. 2......Laws 1839, page....... 234
Stark ....Established Mar. 2....Laws 1839, page....... 229

Ogle, territory added................................... Feb. 22.......Laws 1839, page....... 162
Dane, territory added..................................... Feb. 26.......Laws 1839, page....... 188
Macon, territory added.................... .... Mar. 2......Laws 1839, page....... 265
Hardin-Pope line defined............................ Jan. 8,1840..Laws 1840, page....... 38
Logan, territory added................................ Jan. 29,1840..Laws 1840, page....... 39
Dane, name changed to Christian.................... Feb. 1,1840..Laws 1840, page....... 80

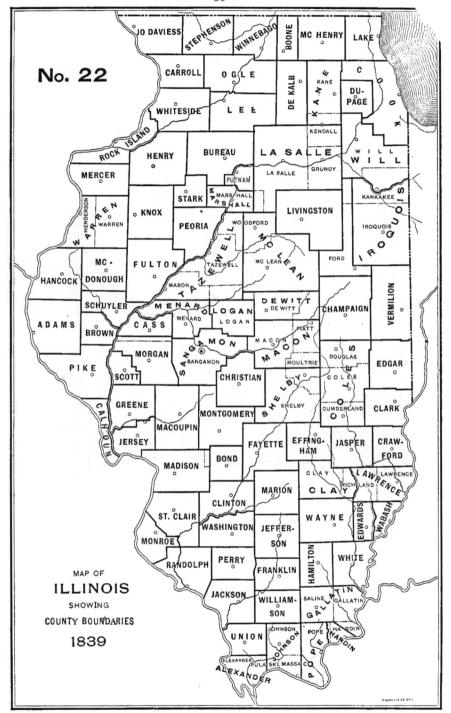

No. 22

MAP OF
ILLINOIS
SHOWING
COUNTY BOUNDARIES
1839

1841-59—FIFTEEN NEW COUNTIES.

Henderson   Established Jan. 20, 1841.................Laws 1841, page..   67
Mason ....Established Jan. 20, 1841.................Laws 1841, page........... 69
Piatt ....Established Jan. 27, 1841.................Laws 1841, page........... 71
Grundy...............Established Feb. 17, 1841.................Laws 1841, page........... 74
Kendall ....Established Feb. 19, 1841.................Laws 1841, page........... 75
Richland ....Established Feb. 24, 1841.................Laws 1841, page........... 77
Woodford ....Established Feb. 27, 1841.................Laws 1841, page............. 84
Massac...............Established Feb. 8 and Mar. 3, 1843....Laws 1843, pages....... 74, 101
Moultrie ....Established Feb. 16, 1843.................Laws 1843, page........... 83
Cumberland ....Established Mar. 2, 1843.................Laws 1843, page........... 94
Pulaski ....Established Mar. 3, 1843.................Laws 1843, page... 99
Saline ....Established Feb. 25, 1847.................Private laws 1847, page ... 34
Kankakee ....Established Feb. 11, 1853.................Laws 1853, page   159
Douglas ....Established Feb. 8 and 16, 1859.........Laws 1859, pages....24 and 28
Ford ....Established Feb. 17, 1859.................Laws 1859, page........... 29

Bond, part of Madison added...................Mar. 2, 1843......Laws 1843, page............ 98
Boone, part of Winnebago added ....Feb. 28, 1843......Laws 1843, page.... 92
Marshall, part of LaSalle added...............Mar. 1, 1843......Laws 1843, page............ 93
Menard, part of Sangamon added ....Mar. 2, 1843......Laws 1843, page...... 94
McHenry, boundary re-defined ....Feb. 28, 1843......Laws 1843, page............ 91
Pope, part of Massac added...................Mar. 3, 1843......Laws 1843, page.... 101
Woodford-McLean, boundary line defined..Feb. 28, 1843......Laws 1843, page............ 91
Cass, part of Morgan added...................Feb. 16, 1845......Laws 1845, page............ 313
Logan, part of DeWitt added.................Feb. 26, 1845......Laws 1845, page............ 189
Peoria-Fulton, boundary defined ....Feb. 28, 1845......Laws 1845, page............ 267
Hardin, part of Gallatin added...............Feb. 20, 1847......Private laws 1847, page 31
Menard, part of Sangamon added ....Feb. 28, 1847......Private laws 1847, page 39
Greene-Jersey, boundary defined............Mar. 3, 1851......Laws 1851, page............ 145
Hamilton-Saline, boundary defined.........Feb. 28, 1854......Laws 1854, page............ 143
White-Gallatin, boundary defined ....Feb. 28, 1854......Laws 1854, page............ 143
Rock Island-Whiteside, boundary defined...Mar. 4, 1854......Laws 1854, page............ 161
Rock Island-Whiteside, repeal ....Mar. 29, 1869......Laws 1869, page............ 161

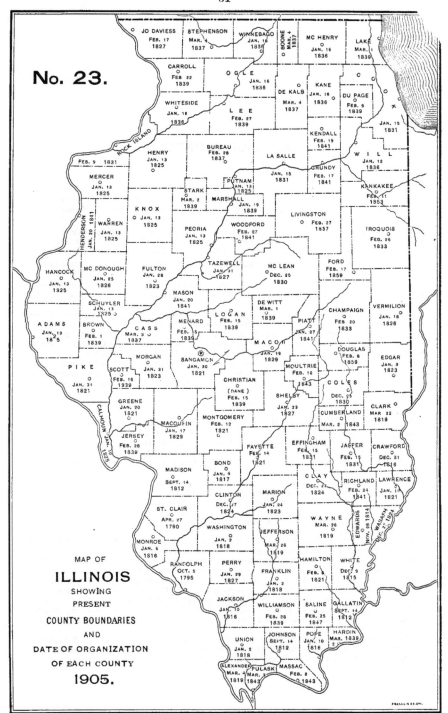

No. 23.

MAP OF
ILLINOIS
SHOWING
PRESENT
COUNTY BOUNDARIES
AND
DATE OF ORGANIZATION
OF EACH COUNTY
1905.

NAMES OF COUNTIES.

Six counties of Illinois, WASHINGTON, JEFFERSON, MADISON, MONROE, ADAMS and JACKSON, were named for Presidents of the United States; ADAMS for John Quincy Adams, sixth President and not for John Adams, second President as is sometimes stated.

Four counties, BOND, COLES, EDWARD and FORD, were named, respectively, for the first, second, third and seventh Governors of Illinois. Bond received its name the year before the election of the first Governor of the State.

Sixteen counties were named for other citizens of the State, prominent in different walks of life.

ALEXANDER, for William M. Alexander, an early settler of the county bearing his name and Senator in the second and third General Assemblies of the State.

COOK, for Daniel P. Cook, a pioneer lawyer, first Attorney General of the State and Representative in Congress from 1819 to 1827.

DOUGLAS, for Stephen A. Douglas, an eminent lawyer, brilliant political orator, Secretary of State (1840), Representative in Congress (1843-1847), United States Senator (1847-1861) and candidate for the Presidency in 1860.

EDGAR, for John Edgar, a pioneer merchant, politician and land speculator.

KANE, for Elias Kent Kane, a pioneer lawyer, Territorial judge, prominent member of the Constitutional Convention of 1818, first Secretary of State of Illinois, and later United States Senator.

LOGAN, for Dr. John Logan, a pioneer physician, father of General John A. Logan.

McHENRY, for William McHenry, a pioneer of White county, soldier of the war of 1812 and the Black Hawk war, Representative in the first, fourth, fifth and ninth General Assemblies, and Senator in the sixth.

McLEAN, for John McLean, a pioneer lawyer, Territorial judge, first representative in Congress from Illinois (1818), and United States Senator (1824-1825).

MENARD, for Pierre Menard, a pioneer Indian trader, Colonel of Territorial militia and first Lieutenant Governor of the State.

OGLE, for Joseph Ogle, pioneer politician and Lieutenant of Territorial militia.

PIATT, for Benjamin Piatt, a pioneer lawyer and Attorney General of the Territory (1810-1813).

POPE, for Nathaniel Pope, first Territorial Secretary of State (1809-1816), and last Territorial Delegate to Congress from Illinois.

STEPHENSON, for Benjamin Stephenson, prominent pioneer, a Colonel of Territorial militia and Adjutant General of the Territory (1813-1814).

WHITE, for Leonard White, pioneer of Gallatin county, Major of Territorial militia, member of Constitutional Convention of 1818, State Senator in second and third General Assemblies, and killed at battle of Tippecanoe Nov. 7, 1811.

WHITESIDE, for Samuel Whiteside, a Colonel of Territorial militia, Representative in the First General Assembly, and Brigadier General of militia during Black Hawk war.

WILL, for Conrad Will, a pioneer politician, Territorial Recorder of Jackson county, member of the Constitutional Convention of 1818, and member of the General Assemblies of the State from the first to ninth, inclusive.

Twenty-two counties were named in honor of military heroes, generally of the Revolution, but some of later wars.

BROWN, for Jacob Brown, Major General during the war of 1812, who won distinction at Sackett's Harbor, Chippewa and Niagara.

CLARK, for George Rogers Clark, a soldier of the Revolution, who, as a Colonel of Virginia militia, established Colonial control in the Illinois country, by the capture of Kaskaskia and Fort Vincennes.

DeKALB, for Johann DeKalb, a German baron, who served in the Colonies during the Revolution, and was mortally wounded at Camden, S. C., 1780.

GREENE, for Nathaniel Greene, a Major General in the Revolution, who distinguished himself as commander in the Southern Colonies.

JASPER, for William Jasper, a Sergeant of the Revolution, who, during the action in Charleston harbor, replaced the flag shot away at Fort Moultrie, and later was killed at Savannah, 1779.

JoDAVIESS, for Joseph Hamilton Daviess, prominent lawyer of Kentucky, United States District Attorney, and major of militia; killed at the battle of Tippecanoe, 1811.

JOHNSON, for Richard M. Johnson, a Colonel of Kentucky militia, who served in Indian wars and the war of 1812, and reputed to have killed the Indian chief, Tecumseh, at the battle of the Thames; Representative in Congress and United States Senator from Kentucky and Vice-President, 1837–1841.

KNOX, for Henry Knox, a soldier of the Revolution who commanded the storming party at Stony Point, later a Major General and Washington's Secretary of War.

MARION, for Francis Marion, a soldier of the Revolution who distinguished himself as a partisan commander in the Carolinas.

MERCER, for Hugh Mercer, a General of the Revolution, killed at the battle of Princeton.

MONTGOMERY, for Richard Montgomery, a Revolutionary General, of Irish birth, who was killed before Quebec, December 31, 1775.

MORGAN, for Daniel Morgan, a General of the Revolution, who, as commander of the " Rifle Brigade," served with distinction at Quebec, Saratoga, the Cowpens and other important engagements.

MOULTRIE, for William Moultrie, a General of the Revolution, who built Fort Moultrie and successfully defended it.

PIKE, for Zebulon Pike, an early explorer of the Louisiana purchase. Pike's Peak was named in his honor. He was a General of the war of 1812 and was killed at York, Canada.

PULASKI, for Count Casimir Pulaski, a Polish exile who espoused the cause of the Colonies during the Revolution and was killed at the attack on Savannah, 1779.

PUTNAM, for Israel Putnam, a Major General of the Revolution.

SCHUYLER, for Philip Schuyler, a soldier of the French and Indian wars, a Major General of the Revolution, a member of the Continental Congress and United States Senator from New York.

STARK, for John Stark, a soldier of the French and Indian wars, a Major General of the Revolution who served with distinction at Bunker Hill, Trenton, Princeton and Bennington.

ST. CLAIR, for Arthur St. Clair, a soldier of the French and In ian wars, a Major General during the Revolution, Commander-in-Chief of the Army after the Revolution, and Governor of the Territory of the United States northwest of the Ohio.

WARREN, for Joseph Warren, a physician and soldier who served at Lexington, a Major General of Massachusetts militia; killed at the battle of Bunker Hill.

WAYNE, for Anthony Wayne, a surveyor and politician of Pennsylvania, a Major General during the Revolution, Commander-in-Chief of the Army after General St. Clair, and successful Indian fighter in the Northwest Territory.

Three counties were named in honor of naval commanders:

LAWRENCE, for Captain James Lawrence, Commander of the Chesapeake, who was mortally wounded in an engagement between that vessel and the British vessel, Shannon, during the war of 1812.

McDONOUGH, for Thomas McDonough, a Commodore of the United States Navy, who commanded the fleet on Lake Champlain in a successful engagement with a British fleet, near Plattsburg, 1814.

PERRY, for Oliver Hazard Perry, a Commodore of the United States Navy, who won distinction as Commander of the fleet in the battle of Lake Erie, in 1813.

Twenty-one counties were named for statesmen and politicians, not citizens of Illinois, some of whom had distinguished themselves in military as well as civil life:

CALHOUN, for John C. Calhoun, a lawyer and statesman, Representative in Congress and United States Senator from South Carolina, Secretary of War under Monroe, Vice President of the United States. and Secretary of State under Tyler, and was recognized as the "Father of Nullification."

CARROLL, for Charles Carroll of Carrollton, a statesman of the Revolutionary period, signer of the Declaration of Independence, and United States Senator from Maryland.

CASS, for Lewis Cass, a soldier as well as statesman, Terrtiorial Governor of Michigan, Minister to France, United States Senator from Michigan, Secretary of War under Jackson, Secretary of State under Buchanan, and at one time a prominent candidate for the Presidency.

CLAY, for Henry Clay, a statesman and political orator, Representative in Congress and United States Senator from Kentucky, three times Speaker of the United States House of Representatives, famous as the author of the political measures known as the "Missouri Compromise," and a prominent. candidate for the Presidency.

CLINTON, for DeWitt Clinton, a distinguished lawyer, financier and statesman, Mayor of the city and Governor of the State of New York, United States Senator, and chief promoter of the Erie Canal.

CRAWFORD, for William H. Crawford of Georgia, United States Senator, Minister to France, Secretary of War, Secretary of the Treasury, and a prominent candidate for the Presidency in 1824.

DEWITT, for DeWitt Clinton. (See Clinton county).

FRANKLIN, for Benjamin Franklin, philosopher, statesman, diplomatist, author, printer, a member of the Continental Congress, Ambassador to France, and (before the Revolution) Deputy Postmaster General of the British Colonies in America.

GALLATIN, for Albert Gallatin, a statesman and financier, Representative in Congress from Pennsylvania, Secretary of the Treasury of the United States, and Minister to France and England.

GRUNDY, for Felix Grundy, a lawyer and politician, United States Senator from Tennessee, and Attorney General of the United States.

HAMILTON, for Alexander Hamilton, a soldier, statesman, author and financier, aid on the staff of Washington during the Revolution, a member of the Continental Congress, first Secretary of the Treasury (1789–1795) and Commander in Chief of the United States Army in 1799.

HANCOCK, for John Hancock, a prominent figure of the Revolutionary period, a Major General of Militia, President of the Continental Congress, first signer of the Declaration, and first Governor of the State of Massachusetts.

HENRY, for Patrick Henry, a lawyer, orator and statesman of the Revolutionary period, a member of the Continental Congress, and Governor of Virginia.

KENDALL, for Amos Kendall, a successful politician and journalist, Postmaster General under Jackson, and as partner of S. F. B. Morse, the inventor of the electric telegraph, he contributed largely to the commercial success of that invention.

LEE, for Richard Henry Lee, an orator and statesman of the Revolutionary period, a member of the Continental Congress, a Representative in Congress and United States Senator from Virginia.

LIVINGSTON, for Edward Livingston, a lawyer and statesman, mayor of New York City, Representative in Congress from New York and later from Louisiana, United States Senator from the latter State, Secretary of State under Jackson, and United States Minister to France

MACON, for Nathaniel. Macon, a Colonel during the Revolution and later a Representative and United States Senator in Congress from North Carolina.

He strenuously opposed the adoption of the United States Constitution as conferring powers on the federal government which should be reserved to the States.

MARSHALL. for John Marshall, a soldier of the Revolution, statesman, author and jurist, Ambassador to France, Representative in Congress from Virginia, Secretary of State and Chief Justice of the United States Supreme Court.

RANDOLPH, for Edmund Randolph, a soldier of the Revolution, a lawyer and statesman, member of the Continental Congress, Attorney General and Gover nor of Virginia. Secretary of State of the United States and Attorney General under Washington.

SHELBY, for Isaac Shelby, a soldier of the Revolution and Indian wars, Governor of Kentucky (1792-1796) and again (1812-1816). He commanded the Kentucky troops in the battle of the Thames in the war of 1812.

TAZEWELL. for Lyttleton W. Tazewell, an eminent lawyer. Governor, Representative in Congress, and United States Senator from Virginia.

Nine counties of Illinois adopted the names of counties of other states through the influence of emigrants from the counties whose names were thus adopted: CHAMPAIGN and RICHLAND from Ohio: CHRISTIAN, HARDIN, HENDERSON, MASON, SCOTT and WOODFORD from Kentucky; and WILLIAMSON from Tennessee.

Seven counties bear Indian names, given originally, as a general rule, to a creek, river or lake, and afterward transferred to the county. These names are IROQUOIS, KANKAKEE, MACOUPIN, PEORIA, SANGAMON, WABASH and WINNEBAGO.

Fourteen other counties derive their names from sources so diverse that they can not easily be classified under any special head.

BOONE, for Daniel Boone, a pioneer hunter, Indian fighter and pathfinder of the early days.

BUREAU, for Pierre Buero, a French trader with the Indians.

CUMBERLAND, from the Cumberland road, named in its turn from the town of Cumberland, Maryland, which derived its name from the mountain range of the same name adopted, presumably, from the Cumberland mountains of Great Britain.

· DU PAGE, from a small river of the same name said to have derived its name from a French trapper and trader of that region.

EFFINGHAM, for Lord Edward Effingham, who· resigned his commission as general in the British army, 1775. refusing to serve in the war against the colonies.

FULTON, for Robert Fulton, the first successful builder of steamboats on American waters.

JERSEY. for the State of New Jersey. which derived its name from the Isle of Jersey, Great Britian.

LAKE. for Lake Michigan.

LA SALLE, for Robert de La Salle, the French explorer who effected the first white settlements in Illinois and explored the Mississippi to the Gulf.

MASSAC. from Fort Massac, a corruption of a French surname, Massiac.

ROCK ISLAND, from a rocky island of that name in the Mississippi.

SALINE. from Saline creek, so called on account of numerous salt springs in that locality.

UNION, for the federal union of the American States.

VERMILION, from the river of that name, the principal branches of which flow through the county

---

NOTE.—The foregoing article and accompanying maps were prepared by Mr. S. L. Spear of the Index department of this office. who wishes to acknowledge his indebtedness to Judge W. L. Gross, of Springfield, for the use of a valuable set of original maps and notes covering the same subject.　　　　　　　　　　JAMES A. ROSE, *Secretary of State.*

—5 C I

LIST OF COUNTIES.

Showing Origin of Name, Date of Organization, County Seat, Area and Population in 1900.

The nineteen counties marked * are not under township organization. The others have adopted township organization.

Counties.	Origin of Name.	Established.	Area— square miles.	County Seat.	Pop 1900
Adams.	John Quincy Adams	Jan. 13,1825	830	Quincy	67,058
*Alexander	William M. Alexander	Mar. 4,1819	220	Cairo	19,384
Bond	Gov. Shadrach Bond	Jan. 4,1817	380	Greenville	16,078
Boone	Daniel Boone	Mar. 4,1837	288	Belvidere	15,791
Brown	Gen. Jacob Brown	Feb. 1,1839	306	Mt. Sterling	11,557
Bureau	Pierre de Buero, Indian trader.	Feb. 28,1837	846	Princeton	41,112
*Calhoun	John C. Calhoun	Jan. 10,1825	251	Hardin	8,917
Carroll	Chas. Carroll, of Carrollton	Feb. 22,1839	450	Mt. Carroll	18,963
*Cass	Gen. Lewis Cass	Mar. 3,1837	460	Virginia	17,222
Champaign	A county in Ohio	Feb. 20,1833	1,008	Urbana	47,622
Christian	A county in Kentucky	Feb. 15,1839	702	Taylorville	32,790
Clark	George Rogers Clark	Mar. 22,1819	513	Marshall	24,033
Clay	Henry Clay	Dec. 23,1824	466	Louisville	19,553
Clinton	De Witt Clinton	Dec. 27,1824	487	Carlyle	19,824
Coles	Gov. Edward Coles	Dec. 25,1830	520	Charleston	34,146
Cook	Daniel P. Cook	Jan. 15,1831	890	Chicago	1,838,735
Crawford	William H. Crawford	Dec. 31,1816	470	Robinson	19,240
Cumberland	Cumberland Road	Mar. 2,1843	350	Toledo	16,124
DeKalb	Baron DeKalb	Mar. 4,1837	650	Sycamore	31,756
DeWitt	DeWitt Clinton	Mar. 1,1839	410	Clinton	18,972
Douglas	Stephen A. Douglas.	Feb. 8,1859	410	Tuscola	19,097
DuPage	DuPage river	Feb. 9,1839	340	Wheaton	28,196
Edgar	John Edgar	Jan. 3,1823	640	Paris	28,273
*Edwards	Gov. Ninian Edwards	Nov. 28,1814	220	Albion	10,345
Effingham	Gen. Edward Effingham	Feb. 15,1831	486	Effingham	20,465
Fayette	Marquis de La Fayette	Feb. 14,1821	720	Vandalia	28,065
Ford	Gov. Thomas Ford	Feb. 17,1859	580	Paxton	18,359
Franklin	Benjamin Franklin	Jan. 2,1818	430	Benton	19,675
Fulton	Robert Fulton	Jan. 28,1823	864	Lewistown	46,201
Gallatin	Albert Gallatin	Sept. 14,1812	310	Shawneetown	15,836
Greene	Gen. Nathaniel Greene	Jan. 20,1821	540	Carrollton	23,402
Grundy	Felix Grundy	Feb. 17,1841	440	Morris	24,136
Hamilton	Alexander Hamilton	Feb. 8,1821	440	McLeansboro	20,197
Hancock	John Hancock	Jan. 13,1825	780	Carthage	32,215
*Hardin	A county in Kentucky	Mar. 2,1839	180	Elizabethtown	7,448
*Henderson	Henderson river	Jan. 20,1841	380	Oquawka	10,836
Henry	Patrick Henry	Jan. 13,1825	825	Cambridge	40,049
Iroquois	Indian name	Feb. 26,1833	1,100	Watseka	38,014
Jackson	Andrew Jackson	Jan. 10,1816	580	Murphysboro	33,871
Jasper	Sergt. William Jasper	Feb. 15,1831	484	Newton	20,160
Jefferson	Thomas Jefferson	Mar. 26,1819	466	Mt. Vernon	28,133
Jersey	New Jersey	Feb. 28,1839	360	Jerseyville	14,612
JoDaviess	Col. Jo Daviess	Feb. 17,1827	650	Galena	24,533
*Johnson	Col. Richard M. Johnson	Sept. 14,1812	340	Vienna	15,667
Kane	Senator Elias K. Kane	Jan. 16,1836	540	Geneva	78,792
Kankakee	Indian name	Feb. 11,1853	680	Kankakee	37,154
Kendall	Amos Kendall	Feb. 19,1841	321	Yorkville	11,467
Knox	Gen. Henry Knox	Jan. 13,1825	720	Galesburg	43,612
Lake	Lake Michigan	Mar. 1,1839	394	Waukegan	34,503
LaSalle	LaSalle, the explorer	Jan. 15,1831	1,152	Ottawa	87,776
Lawrence	Com. James Lawrence	Jan. 16,1821	362	Lawrenceville	16,523
Lee	Richard Henry Lee	Feb. 27,1839	728	Dixon	29,894
Livingston	Edward Livingston	Feb. 27,1837	1,026	Pontiac	42,035

List of Counties—Concluded.

Counties.	Origin of Name.	Established.	Area— square miles.	County Seat.	Pop. 1900
Logan	Dr. John Logan	Feb. 15, 1839	620	Lincoln	28,680
Macon	Nathaniel Macon	Jan. 19, 1829	580	Decatur	44,003
Macoupin	Indian name	Jan. 17, 1829	864	Carlinville	42,256
Madison	James Madison	Sept. 14, 1812	740	Edwardsville	64,694
Marion	Gen. Francis Marion	Jan. 24, 1823	576	Salem	30,446
Marshall	John Marshall	Jan. 19, 1839	350	Lacon	16,370
Mason	A county in Kentucky	Jan. 20, 1841	518	Havana	17,491
*Massac	Fort Massac	Feb. 8, 1843	240	Metropolis	13,110
McDonough	Com. Thomas McDonough	Jan. 25, 1826	576	Macomb	28,412
McHenry	Gen. William McHenry	Jan. 16, 1836	612	Woodstock	29,759
McLean	John McLean	Dec. 25, 1830	1,161	Bloomington	67,843
*Menard	Pierre Menard	Feb. 15, 1839	311	Petersburg	14,336
Mercer	Gen. Hugh Mercer	Jan. 13, 1825	550	Aledo	20,945
*Monroe	James Monroe	Jan. 6, 1816	380	Waterloo	13,847
Montgomery	Gen. Richard Montgomery	Feb. 12, 1821	740	Hillsboro	30,836
*Morgan	Gen. Daniel Morgan	Jan. 31, 1823	563	Jacksonville	35,006
Moultrie	Gen. William Moultrie	Feb. 16, 1843	340	Sullivan	15,224
Ogle	Lieut. Joseph Ogle	Jan. 16, 1836	773	Oregon	29,129
Peoria	Indian name	Jan. 13, 1825	630	Peoria	88,608
*Perry	Com. Oliver H. Perry	Jan. 29, 1827	432	Pinckneyville	19,830
Piatt	Benjamin Piatt	Jan. 27, 1841	440	Monticello	17,706
Pike	Zebulon M. Pike	Jan. 31, 1821	756	Pittsfield	31,595
*Pope	Nathaniel Pope	Jan. 10, 1816	360	Golconda	13,585
*Pulaski	Count Casimir Pulaski	Mar. 3, 1843	190	Mound City	14,554
Putnam	Gen. Israel Putnam	Jan. 13, 1825	170	Hennepin	4,746
*Randolph	Edmund Randolph	Oct. 5, 1795	560	Chester	28,001
Richland	A county in Ohio	Feb. 24, 1841	380	Olney	16,391
Rock Island	Island of same name	Feb. 9, 1831	420	Rock Island	55,249
Saline	Saline creek	Feb. 25, 1847	396	Harrisburg	21,685
Sangamon	Indian name	Jan. 30, 1821	875	Springfield	71,593
Schuyler	Gen. Philip Schuyler	Jan. 13, 1825	414	Rushville	16,129
*Scott	A county in Kentucky	Feb. 16, 1839	252	Winchester	10,455
Shelby	Gov. Isaac Shelby	Jan. 23, 1827	760	Shelbyville	32,126
Stark	Gen. John Stark	Mar. ?, 1839	290	Toulon	10,186
St. Clair	Gen. Arthur St. Clair	April 27, 1790	680	Belleville	86,685
Stephenson	Col. Benjamin Stephenson	Mar. 4, 1837	573	Freeport	31,288
Tazewell	Gov. Lyttleton W. Tazewell	Jan. 31, 1827	650	Pekin	33,221
*Union	The Union	Jan. 2, 1818	400	Jonesboro	22,610
Vermilion	Vermilion river	Jan. 18, 1826	882	Danville	65,635
*Wabash	Indian name	Dec. 27, 1824	220	Mt. Carmel	12,583
Warren	Gen. Joseph Warren	Jan. 13, 1825	540	Monmouth	23,163
Washington	George Washington	Jan. 2, 1818	557	Nashville	19,526
Wayne	Gen. Anthony Wayne	Mar. 26, 1819	720	Fairfield	27,626
White	Capt. Leonard White	Dec. 9, 1815	500	Carmi	25,386
Whiteside	Col. Samuel Whiteside	Jan. 16, 1836	676	Morrison	34,710
Will	Conrad Will	Jan. 12, 1836	850	Joliet	74,764
*Williamson	A county in Tennessee	Feb. 28, 1839	440	Marion	27,796
Winnebago	Indian name	Jan. 16, 1836	540	Rockford	47,845
Woodford	A county in Kentucky	Feb. 27, 1841	556	Eureka	21,822

Lightning Source UK Ltd.
Milton Keynes UK
UKHW02f1815010818
326639UK00012B/449/P